LAST WORDS SERIES

Life, Death & Last Words of
JOHN KEATS

DR. ANUP KUMAR CHANDA

BLUEROSE PUBLISHERS
India | U.K.

Copyright © Dr Anup Kumar Chanda 2023

All rights reserved by author. No part of this publication may be reproduced, stored in a retrieval system or transmitted in any form or by any means, electronic, mechanical, photocopying, recording or otherwise, without the prior permission of the author. Although every precaution has been taken to verify the accuracy of the information contained herein, the publisher assume no responsibility for any errors or omissions. No liability is assumed for damages that may result from the use of information contained within.

BlueRose Publishers takes no responsibility for any damages, losses, or liabilities that may arise from the use or misuse of the information, products, or services provided in this publication.

For permissions requests or inquiries regarding this publication, please contact:

BLUEROSE PUBLISHERS
www.BlueRoseONE.com
info@bluerosepublishers.com
+91 8882 898 898
+4407342408967

ISBN: 978-93-5989-991-6

Cover design: Tahira
Typesetting: Tanya Raj Upadhyay

First Edition: December 2023

To,

Sourabh, Sagnika, Pakhi

&

My loving wife Dhriti

who loved her children a lot.

"I think I shall be among the English poets after my death."

*--- John Keats to his brother George,
in a letter dated October 14, 1818*

Preface

William Butler Yeats, called him *"the coarse-bred son of a livery stable keeper"* who produced *"luxuriant song."*

" ... you are capable of the greatest things ..., Shelley thought of him.

"... since my childhood I have loved none better than your marvellous kinsman, that godlike boy, the real Adonis of our age. ... In my heaven he walks eternally with Shakespeare and the Greeks," Oscar Wilde, the aestheticist non-pareil wrote of him after his death.

Despite such lofty praises showered on him, his *"luxuriant songs"* were damned by the critics, particularly after publication his first major work *"Endymion"*, a four-thousand-line allegorical romance based on the Greek myth of the same name, when a harsh review by John Wilson Croker appeared in the April 1818 edition of the '*Quarterly Review*'. Alongside, John Gibson Lockhart of '*Blackwood's Magazine*', described '*Endymion*' as "*the calm, settled, imperturbable drivelling idiocy*". With biting sarcasm, he advised,

> *"It is a better and a wiser thing to be a starved apothecary than a starved poet; so back to the shop Mr. John, back to plasters, pills, and ointment boxes."*

Incredible it may seem today, the victim of the toxic attack as above was none other than John Keats, only a budding poet then, who later came to be recognised as one of the greatest English Romantic poets ever. Fortunately for English literature, Keats, ignored the rude and spiteful advice of his namesake, critic John Lockhart; no doubt he was deeply hurt within, but he refused to go back to the world of *"plasters, pills, and ointment boxes"* as suggested by his biased and malicious critics, and preferred to be a *"starved poet"*.

Keats died at the tragically early age of 25. At the time of his death, his admirers praised him for having developed a style more heavily loaded with sensualities, gorgeous in its effects and sprightly alive to realities compared to any earlier poet. All his poems have a charming silken weighty expression;

they are, to use one of his own phrases, *"more of an artist, and load every rift* [of the subject] *with ore."* [1]

Despite their irresistible appeal, initially there was only a very small group of readers for his poems. Alongside, the sustained vicious attacks against his work by a section of critics, particularly from the influential magazines, like, *'Quarterly Review'* and *'Blackwood Magazine'*, also limited the sale of his books adversely influencing the general readers against his work. As a result, at the time of his death, the combined sales of Keats's three volumes of poetry published during his lifetime is estimated to be only 200 copies.

****

At the time of his death, Keats had been writing poetry seriously for only about six years, from 1814 until the summer of 1820, and publishing for only four years. His first poem, the sonnet *'O Solitude! if I must with thee dwell'*, was published in the liberal weekly *'Examiner'*, edited by the well-known radical Leigh Hunt who grouped Keats together with Percy Bysshe Shelley and John Hamilton Reynolds as three young writers who promised a *"considerable addition of strength"* to a new school. Hunt also introduced Keats to a group of eminent poets, including Shelley and William Wordsworth. The group's influence enabled Keats to see his first volume, *"Poems"*, published in 1817.

Ironically, however, it was because of his association with Hunt and his principles in poetry and politics, Keats's literary work during his lifetime, even after publication of his first major work *"Endymion"*, was subject to most unkind and notorious critical attack ever on a living poet in the British literary history. Calling the romantic verse of Hunt's literary circle *"the Cockney school of poetry,"* the influential *"Blackwood's Magazine"* declared *Endymion* to be nonsense. In particular, Lockhart, the critic of the *"Blackwood's Magazine"*, relentlessly satirised Keats's stylistic mannerism. His attack, basically a toxic mix of social sneering, personal insult and outrageously wilful bias, began with some swipes at Keats's first book titled

---

[1] *"You, I am sure, will forgive me for sincerely remarking that you might curb your magnanimity, and be more of an artist, and load every rift of your subject with ore."* This was Keats's friendly advice in a letter he wrote to Shelley on August 16th 1820: The letter was in response to Shelley's invitation for Keats to spend the winter at his home in Pisa, Italy after finding out Keats was ill with tuberculosis. [See, Schuster, Lincoln M., *"The World's great Letters"*, Simon & Schuster, New York, 1940, pp.240-241.

"*Poems 1817*", published on 3 March 1817, before settling to sustained deriding of "*Endymion*" published in 1818. The dismissal was more class-based than literary, maliciously aimed at young writers like him not from the upper classes deemed uncouth for their lack of education at Eton, Harrow or Oxbridge, their non-conventional rhyming and "low diction". A major cause of Keats's premature death, it is widely believed, was such vitriolic attacks by his critics; he was so embittered with life that he did not even desire to have his name on his epitaph. All he wished was that just the following phrase be inscribed on his tombstone after his death, "*Here lies one whose name was writ in water.*"

Keats is buried in the Protestant Cemetery, Rome, Italy, which is now one of the highlights of a trip to Rome. His grave is in a quiet corner with his painter friend Joseph Severn, who accompanied him to Rome and nursed him till the last moment, buried next to him.

****

By the time his death arrived, Keats was mentally devasted. He died on 23 February, 1821; by then he had lost all hope and believed he would soon be forgotten. So, all he wanted to be inscribed on his tombstone was "*Here lies one whose name was writ in water.*" He didn't even wish his name in his epitaph; merely this line. But just less than two and half years ago, he was full of energy and vigour, with sky-kissing ambition, and dream in his eyes. He was confident that for his literary work, he will be remembered by the posterity. He was so passionate about poetry that in 1818, he dared to leave the safe and secure pursuit as an apothecary and opted for the uncertain pasture of a poet. The same year, in one of his letters to his brother George on the 14th October to his brother George, he had confidently stated, "*I think I shall be among the English poets after my death.*"

Keats's prediction about being recognized among English poets after his death ultimately came true, as he is now widely regarded as one of the leading figures of the Romantic movement and a master of poetic expression. His poetry continues to inspire and resonate with readers around the world.

Keats's statement "*I think I shall be among the English poets after my death*" stands as a testament to his artistic conviction and foresight. Through his poetic genius and unwavering belief in his work, he secured a place among the great English poets and became an eternal voice in the annals of literature.

As we continue to cherish and celebrate his legacy, we are reminded that the words of a poet can indeed live on, touching the souls of generations far beyond their own time.

****

Keats was suffering from tuberculosis. As his condition worsened, he was advised by his doctors to avoid the English winter and go to a sunny place like, Italy. But before he actually set out for Rome to catch some sunshine, Keats had fallen in love with a young woman named Fanny Brawne. Their passionate and intense love story is well-documented through their letters and poems, and it remains one of the most memorable romances in literary history. In one of his letters to her, he wrote: "*My love is selfish. I cannot breathe without you.*" [2]

Keats first met Fanny in the autumn of 1818 when she moved into the house next door to his residence in Hampstead, London. Keats was already an established poet, while Fanny was an 18-year-old vivacious and stylish young woman, and her charm captivated Keats from the very beginning. It was a love at first sight and their relationship soon blossomed into a romantic one over time. Their love was not without obstacles. Keats was struggling financially and his literary work faced constant criticism from a section of critics, which took a toll on his emotional well-being. Nevertheless, he found solace and inspiration in his love for Fanny, often expressing his feelings through poetry.

One of Keats's most famous love poems is "*Bright Star*," which many believe was written for Fanny. The poem reflects his yearning for a stable and enduring love amidst the uncertainties of his life:

Their love was genuine and profound, but it faced numerous challenges. Not long after they met, Keats's health began to decline, and he was diagnosed with tuberculosis in 1820. Despite the crisis, Fanny remained devoted to Keats and remained by his side as best she could. In late 1820, on doctor's advice, Keats had to leave England to travel to Italy in search of a warmer climate to improve his health, leaving behind the love of his life. Fanny

---

[2] Keats, John: "*Bright Star: Love Letters and Poems of John Keats to Fanny Brawne*", Penguin Books; Media Tie In edition, 16 September 2009.

remained in England, and they exchanged letters, but they never saw each other again.

Keats passed away in Rome on February 23, 1821, at the young age of 25, far away from Fanny. Only the letters and poems they exchanged remain behind as poignant reminders of their deep love and affection for each another.

The love between John Keats and Fanny Brawne has become a moving symbol of true love and enduring passion, immortalized not only in their personal letters but also in Keats's immortal poetry. Their story continues to captivate readers and inspire romantic souls to this day.

****

Keats was an early nineteenth century poet. What is his relevance in today's world?

Well, more than two centuries have passed since the death of John Keats, but his poetry and other literary works continue to resonate with the modern audiences and remain relevant still today for several reasons. Here are some aspects of Keats's relevance today:

Timeless Themes: Keats explored universal themes in his poetry, such as love, beauty, nature, and the transience of life. These themes are still relevant to contemporary readers, as they touch upon fundamental aspects of the human experience that transcend time.

Sensory and Emotional Richness: Keats's poetry is known for its vivid imagery and emotional depth. His ability to evoke strong emotions and create sensory experiences through words is admired even in the present day.

Focus on Nature: Keats had a profound appreciation for nature and its ability to inspire awe and wonder. In an increasingly urbanized world, his celebration of nature's beauty and its capacity to heal the soul still holds significant, reminding us of the ever-enchanting appeal of what we miss in our everyday life today.

Pursuit of Aesthetics: Keats was deeply interested in the concept of beauty and the role of art in capturing its essence. In an age where aesthetics, art, and the appreciation of beauty remain significant in various forms, Keats's exploration of these ideas remains pertinent.

Escapism and Imagination: Keats's poetry offers an escape from the mundane and help us undertake a journey into the realms of imagination. In a world full of challenges, his works provide a sanctuary for the imagination to roam freely.

Human Connection: Keats's letters and poems often explore the depth of human relationships and the value of empathy. In an era of technological connectivity, his emphasis on genuine human connection and understanding is a crucial reminder.

In summary, John Keats's relevance today lies in the timelessness of his themes, the emotional resonance of his poetry, his appreciation of nature, and his enduring influence on literature and the arts. His work continues to speak to the human experience, providing solace, inspiration, and a deeper understanding of ourselves and the world around us. An understanding and familiarity with of the life history of the poet can help us better in the matter of appreciation of his poetry and other literary works. Hence this book.

****

This book is dedicated to our son-in-law Sourabh, daughter Sagnika (Doel), granddaughter Jonaki (Pakhi) and to my loving wife Dhriti, who loved her children a lot.

I am indebted to my parents, Late Bibhuti Bhusan Chanda and Late Binapani Chanda for their constant love, affection and support in my life, that made me what I'm today, and gave me the courage to undertake new ventures in life. I also gratefully acknowledge the constant encouragement I received from my elder brother Shri Pradip Kumar Chanda, without which this book would not have been possible.

Last but not the least, I owe my gratitude to my dear friend Shri Baidyanath Mukhopadhyay for his generous help and assistance by meticulously going through the entire manuscript and making several valuable suggestions for improvement.

With this, let me introduce the present book, the second in the "*Last Word Series*", on the tragic "*Life, Death and Last Words*" of John Keats, the nineteenth century English Romantic poet, whose poetry and literary works, characterized by its sensuous imagery, exploration of beauty and mortality, and a profound connection with nature, continue to be widely read and appreciated to this day.

27 September, 2023 (Dr. Anup Kumar Chanda)

Prologue

His Last Words

"Severn—lift me up—I am dying—I shall die easy—don't be frightened—be firm, and thank God it has come!"

In 1818, John Keats returned home from a tour of Northern England and Scotland to care for his brother, Tom, who had contracted tuberculosis. Unfortunately, Tom died in December that year. By that time Keats himself had contracted the disease and as a student of medicine, he knew that his death was imminent.

There was really no good cure for tuberculosis at that time. His doctor advised him to avoid the chilling English cold and seek a warm climate somewhere else, particularly for the winter. Following his doctor's advice, Keats boarded the sailing brig *Maria Crowther* with his friend, the artist Joseph Severn, on September 17, 1820 and reached Rome on November 14, 1820. On reaching Rome, he recovered briefly for Christmas but in January, 1821, there was a slow and steady decline into the final stage of tuberculosis. Keats was unable to leave his bedroom. He was coughing up blood and covered in sweat; he was unable to leave his bedroom.

Severn nursed him devotedly. But his condition rapidly deteriorated. On February 23, 1821, a little before mid-night, Keats died peacefully in Severn's arms. Even while dying, he sought to comfort Severn:

"Severn—lift me up—I am dying—I shall die easy—don't be frightened—be firm, and thank God it has come!"

These were his last words.

Not his last words

There is, however, another version of Keats's last words. Some authors claim just before Keats's death, Severn asked the poet how he was doing, to which Keats quietly replied:

> *"Better, my friend, I feel the daisies growing over me."*

But it is not factually correct.

Actually as he lay in critical condition in Rome, Keats wrote a few last lines to console his friend Severn *"who had never seen anyone die"*:

> *"I shall soon be laid in the quiet grave*
> *thank God for the quiet grave*
> *O! I can feel the cold earth upon me*
> *the daisies growing over me*
> *O for this quiet*
> *it will be my first."*

These are beautiful words; but these are not his last words.[3]

Epitaph

Keats is buried in the Protestant Cemetery, Rome, Italy, which is now one of the highlights of a trip to Rome. His grave is in a quiet corner with his friend Joseph Severn buried next to him.

The inscription on the headstone of his tomb reads:

> *"This Grave*
> *contains all that was Mortal*
> *of a*
> *Young English Poet,*
> *Who,*
> *on his Death Bed,*
> *in the Bitterness of his Heart,*
> *at the Malicious Power of his Enemies,*
> *Desired*
> *these Words to be engraven on his Tomb Stone:*
> *HERE LIES ONE WHOSE NAME WAS WRIT IN WATER.*
> *th*
> *Feb 24 1821"*

---

[3] Montague, John: *"A poet pursued by death"*, Irish Times, October 20, 2012.

Keats desired only the phrase *"Here lies one whose name was writ in water"* inscribed on his tombstone. He did not even want his name to appear on his tombstone; merely this line.

The rest of the inscription was added by his friend Severn, who nursed him during his illness, and Keats's closest friend, Charles Brown. Both were grief-stricken and embittered by the critical treatment of Keats's poetry by a section of contemporary critics.

James Clark, his attending doctor in Rome, saw to the planting of daisies on the grave, saying that Keats would have wished it. And, there is also a small plaque on the cemetery wall nearby, on which the following is written:

"K-eats! if thy cherished name be "writ in water"

E-ach drop has fallen from some mourner's cheek;

A-sacred tribute; such as heroes seek,

T-hough oft in vain - for dazzling deeds of slaughter

S-leep on! Not honoured less for Epitaph so meek!"

Seven weeks after the funeral, his friend, Percy Bysshe Shelley, composed the poem *"Adonais"*[4][5] in his memory.

---

[4] Shelley did not hear of the death of Keats in Rome, in February 1821, until some weeks later. The relations between the two were not close. They had met and there had been a few letters exchanged. Shelley had shown sympathy and concern when he learned of Keats's intention to go to Italy for his health and had invited him to be his guest. Shelley also knew of the attacks of the reviewers on Keats's poetry. His own poetry had fared no better than Keats's at the hands of the Tory reviewers. When the report of Keats's death reached him, he was convinced that Keats had been hounded to death by the reviewers, so he decided to write a defence of Keats and an attack on the Tory reviewers. The result was Adonais, which Shelley wrote in the spring and published in the fall of 1821.

To make doubly clear his aggressive intention in the poem, Shelley provided it with a preface in which he called the Tory reviewers "wretched men" and "literary prostitutes." The reviewer of Keats's Endymion in the Quarterly was accused of murder. Adonais and its preface brought down on Shelley the wrath of the conservative reviewers. Blackwood's Magazine attacked him with special savagery. The reception of Adonais deepened Shelley's despairing conviction that he had failed as a poet. He wrote on January 25, 1822, to Leigh Hunt: "*My faculties are shaken to atoms . . . I can write nothing; and if Adonais had no success, and excited no interest what incentive can I have to write?*"

[5] Shelley gave his elegy a title that pointed clearly to his intention to attack the reviewers. Adonais, in Greek mythology, was a beautiful young man. Aphrodite, the goddess of love, fell in love with him. But unfortunately Adonis was killed by a boar; Likewise, 'Adonais' (a variant

"Adonais"

"I weep for Adonais—he is dead!
Oh, weep for Adonais! though our tears
Thaw not the frost which binds so dear a head!
And thou, sad Hour, selected from all years
To mourn our loss, rouse thy obscure compeers,
And teach them thine own sorrow, say: "With me
Died Adonais; till the Future dares
Forget the Past, his fate and fame shall be
An echo and a light unto eternity!"
[Percy B. Shelley, 'Adonais', Stanza I]

Shelley died just one year after Keats, and was buried in the same Protestant Cemetery, Rome, where Keats is buried.

John Keats

The villa on the Spanish Steps in Rome, where Keats breathed his last, is now the *"Keats-Shelly Memorial"* museum -- a pilgrimage for tourists to pay

---

of Adonis coined by Shelley) was killed by reviewers. It was in the tradition of elegy to use proper names taken from classical literature. Shelley's coinage may have been intended to forestall the misapprehension that the poem was about Adonis. Adonais was close enough to serve his purpose. [Source: *'Adonis'*, Shelley's Poems, CliffsNotes]

homage to the two great English bards who died far away from where their hearts truly belonged –England, their sweet home, the "*nest of the singing birds*".

Table of Contents

Preface v
Prologue xii
    His Last Words xii
    Not his last words xii
    Epitaph xiii
Chapter 1 John Keats 1
    Imitation of Spenser" (1814) 4
Chapter 2 Keats meets Leigh Hunt: A Turning point in the History of Literature 7
    "Sonnet On Peace' (1814) 10
    "Lines written on 29 May/ The Anniversary of the Restoration of Charles the 2nd" (1814 or 1815) 11
    "O Solitude! if I must with thee dwell" (1816) 12
Chapter 3 Keats: in love 16
    "To Fanny" (1819) 16
    Isabella Jones: Hush, hush! tread softly! (1818) 17
    Fanny Brawne 18
Chapter 4 1819: Annus Mirabilis 22
Chapter 5 December 20, 1819: Keats hesitates on the threshold of a career in business 25
    "…Tea Brokerage … will not suit me" 26
Chapter 6 Keats: Early Works 28
    1816: "On First Looking into Chapman's Homer" 28
    Keats's First Book: 'Poems' (1817) 30
    Endymion (1818) 31
    Keats: A victim of his critics 33

Chapter 7 Keats: Masterpieces 36
Isabella, or the Pot of Basil (1817-18) 36
The Eve of St. Agnes (1819) 38
The Legend of St. Agnes 40
The Plot 41
Critique 42

Chapter 8 Keats: More Masterpieces I 45
Hyperion (1819) 45
Plot 46
Critique 48

Chapter 9 Keats: More Masterpieces II 52
"La Belle Dame Sans Merci" ("The Beautiful Lady Without Mercy") (1819) 52

Chapter 10 Keats: More Masterpieces III 58
Lamia (1819) 58
Influence 61
"Sonnet -- To Science" (1829) By Edgar Allan Poe 62
Beauty through the lens of science: "…Do I see less or more?" 62
"Ode to a Flower" (1981) 65
Richard Feynman" 65

Chapter 11 Keats: 1819 Odes 66
Why should we explore Keats's Odes separately from his other works? 67
Ode on a Grecian Urn 68
Ode to Psyche 70
Ode to a Nightingale 73
Ode on Melancholy 75
Ode on Indolence 77
To Autumn 81
The subliminal 84

Chapter 12 John Keats & Other Great English Romantic Poets of the 19th Century: **86**
    John Keats and Percy Bysshe Shelley 86
    How close were Shelley and Keats? 86
    December 1816: Keats meets Shelley 87
    "The Mask of Anarchy" (1819) 89

Chapter 13 John Keats & Other Great English Romantic Poets of the 19th Century (Contd.): **91**
    John Keats and Lord George Gordon Byron 91
    Who killed John Keats? -- Excerpts from the Letter of Lord Byron to John Murray, July 30, 1821, shortly after the death of John Keats 93
    "Don Juan" (1821) 96

Chapter 14 Letters of John Keats (1816-21) **98**
    The Importance of the Letters 100
    "Negative Capability" 101
    "Chameleon Poet" 101
    "The Vale of Soul-Making" 102
    "Mansion of Many Apartments" 103
    "Truth is Beauty" 104
    Genius: T.S. Eliot 105

Chapter 15 Keats & Fanny Brawne: Love unbounded **106**
    Between September and November 1818: Keats meets Fanny 106
    Keats and Fanny: Love at first sight 107
    "Shall I give you Miss Brawn[e]?" : Keats writes to his brother and sister-in-law in a letter dated December 25, 1818 108
    Keats on a creative spree – with Fanny as his muse 109

Chapter 16 Love Letters of John Keats **112**
    July 3, 1819 112
    October 1819: Keats returns to Hampstead & meets Fanny after three months' absence: "you dazzled me" 115
    Keats: uncomfortable with women and hoped he'll never marry 115
    July 18, 1818": "I have not a right feeling towards women" 115
    October 25, 1818: "...I hope I shall never marry." 117

October 13, 1819: Keats to Fanny: "Love is my religion" 120

Chapter 17 More Love Letters of John Keats (1820) 122

    4 (?) February, 1820: "The consciousness that you love me will make a pleasant prison of the house next to yours." 122

    10 (?) February 1820: "You had a just right to be a little silent to one who speaks so plainly to you." 123

    (?) February 1820: "I read your note in bed last night, and that might be the reason of my sleeping so much better." 124

    (?) March, 1820: "Even if you did not love me I could not help an entire devotion to you: how much more deeply then must I feel for you knowing you love me." 125

    (?) March 1820: "I envied Sam's walk with you to day; which I will not do again as I may get very tired of envying." 126

    Failing health makes him bitter and jealous: Keats accuses Fanny of flirtation with his friend Charles Brown 126

    July 5, 1820 "Love is not a plaything" 127

    Adieu Fanny: Keats prepares to leave for Rome 129

Chapter 18 Shelley invites Keats to join him in Italy 132

    John Keats acknowledges the invitation to visit Shelley at Pisa 135

    "My imagination is a monastery, and I am its monk …." 135

Chapter 19 On board the 'Maria Crowther': Keats sails for Italy 138

    His Last Will 138

    September 17, 1820: Keats on board the sailing brig 'Maria Crowther' 139

Chapter 20 Keats's Last Sonnet: "Bright Star" 141

    Bright Star 141

    'Bright Star': Who's the Star? Fanny Brawne or Isabella Jones? 145

Chapter 21 Keats arrives at Naples 147

    October 21, 1820: At Naples 147

    November 1, 1820, Keats's letter to Charles Brown: "Was I born for this end?" 148

Chapter 22 The Death of Adonais 150

    November 14, 1820: In Rome 150

November 30, 1820, His Last letter: "... I am leading a posthumous existence." 151

His last wish 153

His last words 154

Chapter 23 Doctor's blunders to blame for Keats's agonising death?: A Controversy 156

Death of John Keats: Controversy 157

"Is the Criticism of John Keats's Doctor Justified? A Bicentenary Re-Appraisal 160

Keats's treatment in Rome 161

Clark's Treatment of Keats: A Critical Analysis 164

Was it a prudent decision for Keats to travel all the way to Rome just for a bit of sunshine? 166

Chapter 24 Death Mask of John Keats 168

Death Mask 168

Life Mask of John Keats 170

Chapter 25 Burial 173

Adonais 175

Chapter 26 The Tomb of John Keats: Through the eyes of Oscar Wilde (1877) 178

'Irish Monthly', July 5, 1877: "The Tomb of John Keats" 178

HEU MISERANDE PUER[]](Hello, Poor Boy) 181

Chapter 27 Fanny learns of Keats's death 183

Chapter 28 1885: Sale by auction of Keats's love-letters 187

December 8, 1865: London Times, Front page 187

Love made public 189

"On The Sale By Auction Of Keats's Love Letters" 189

Chapter 29 March, 2011: Keats's love letter to Fanny sold at auction for £96, 000. 192

In An Auction Room (Letter of John Keats to Fanny Brawne) Anderson Galleries, March 15, 1920 192

1 (?) March, 1820: "I shall kiss your name and mine where your Lips have been…" 193

Chapter 30 Fanny Brawne: Posthumous controversy *195*
   Fanny: Unworthy of Keats's affection and love – Critics 195
   Fanny Brawne's letters to Fanny Keats 197
   Fanny Brawne: A Tailpiece 201

Chapter 31 John Keats: Recognition after death *202*
   "To Autumn" 202
   "Keats-Shelley Memorial House", Rome 203
   During World War II 206

Chapter 32 Epilogue *209*
   In remembrance 209

References *211*

Chapter 1
John Keats

Early Years

"[John] feared that he should never be a poet, & if he was not he would destroy himself"

-- **George Keats, younger brother of John Keats**

A Romantic poet of the second generation of Romanticism, like, Percy B. Shelly and Lord Byron, the poetry of John Keats is characterised by sensual imagery, most notably in his series of odes. By the end of the 19th century, Keats became one of the most beloved of all English poets.

According to some biographers, when Keats became a published poet, he felt his earlier works were not up to the mark; so he burnt them.

Keats was born in Moorgate, London in 1795. Slender and short, just over 5 feet in height, with his reddish-brown curly hair, he was the eldest of the four surviving children of his parents. Throughout his life, Keats had close emotional ties with to his sister, Frances (Fanny) and his two brothers, George and Tom.

Keats's father, Thomas, first worked as an ostler[6] at the stables attached to the Swan and Hoop Inn owned by his father-in-law, John Jennings, and later owned it. The family as such was just about able to manage themselves. Keats believed he was born at the inn, a birthplace of humble origins, though there is no evidence to support this.[7] In April 1804, Thomas died of a skull fracture, when he fell from his horse. Keats was only

---

[6] A hostler or 'ostler' was traditionally a groom or stableman who was employed in a stable to take care of horses, usually at an inn, in the era of transportation by horse or horse-drawn carriage.

[7] Everest, Kelvin: "*Keats, John (1795–1821)*", Oxford Dictionary of National Biography, Oxford University Press, 2004 Online.

eight years old then. The shock to the family was great, both emotionally and financially.

Within a year of his father's death, his mother Frances Jennings remarried a minor bank clerk named William Rawlings. But the marriage proved to be a disaster. After losing the stable and some of her inheritance to her estranged husband, Keats's mother left the family leaving her four children at Edmonton to be looked after by their grandmother. Ten-year-old Keats was traumatized. He began suffering from anxiety attacks, the first of many illnesses (some real, some hypochondriac) that would plague him through his short life. Her mother later returned in 1809, broken and ill, suffering from rheumatism and tuberculosis. He nursed his mother through her illness, but she died in March 1810. leaving the children in the custody of their grandmother.

John Keats

Keats attended a school in the village of Enfield, two miles away, run by John Clarke, whose son Charles Cowden Clarke did much to encourage Keats's literary aspirations. Separated by only eight years, they became close friends; it was Charles who introduced young Keats to the poetry of Edmund Spenser and the Elizabethans. At school Keats was noted as a recalcitrant pupil and was considered "*not literary*", rather a volatile character "*always in extremes*", given to indolence and fighting. However at 13 he began focusing his energy towards reading and study, winning his first academic prize in midsummer 1809.

After the death of his mother in 1810, his grandmother put the children's affairs into the hands of a guardian, Richard Abbey. Abbey also became executor of their grandmother's estate when she died in 1814.

Abbey, however, strongly disregarded the interests and welfare of the children as he often withheld money from their grandmother's estate.[8] He had little interest in the children, and even less in their education. At Abbey's prompting, in 1811, after finishing school, Keats, despite his keen interest in poetry, became an apprentice of a surgeon-apothecary with Thomas Hammond who was their neighbour, and lodged in the attic above the surgery at 7 Church Street until 1813. Cowden Clarke, who remained a close friend of Keats, described this as "*the most placid time in Keats's life*".

On completion of his apprenticeship with Hammond, Keats registered for a study course at Guy's Hospital (now part of King's College), London to become a licensed surgeon-apothecary. He began studying there since October 1815. Keats lodged near the hospital at 28 St Thomas's Street in Southwark, with other medical students; Within a month of starting, he was accepted as a dresser at the hospital, assisting surgeons during operations, the equivalent of a junior house surgeon today. It was a significant promotion marking a distinct aptitude for medicine, the position bringing him increased responsibility and workload. His long and expensive medical training with Hammond and at Guy's Hospital led his family to assume that it would be his lifelong career, assuring financial security, and it seems that at this point Keats had a genuine desire to become a doctor; and he was indeed doing very well in medicine; but it took up increasing amounts of his writing time.

---

[8] From 1814 Keats had two bequests held in trust for him until his 21st birthday: £800 willed by his grandfather John Jennings (about £34,000 in today's money) and a portion of his mother's legacy, £8000 (about £340,000 today), to be equally divided between her living children. It seems Keats was not told of either, since he never applied for any of the money. The blame would naturally go to Abbey as legal guardian, but he may also well have been unaware.

William Walton, solicitor for Keats's mother and grandmother, definitely did know and had a duty of care to relay the information to Keats. It seems he did not carry out his obligation. The money would have surely made a critical difference to the poet's expectations. Money was always a great concern and difficulty for him, as he struggled to stay out of debt and make his way in the world independently. [Source: "*John Keats*", Poemhunters.com]

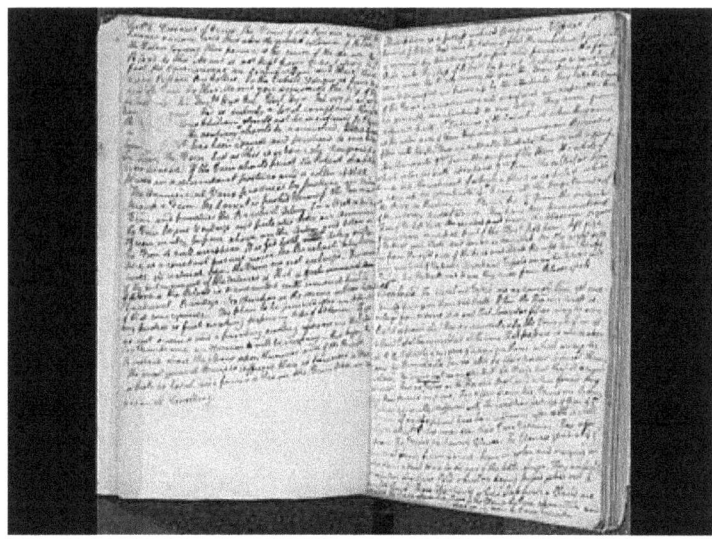

Keats Medical Notebook,
Keats House Museum, Hampstead

At this juncture, Keats was faced with a stark choice. His first surviving poem, "*Imitation of Spenser*", had been written earlier in 1814, when Keats was 19.[9] He was genuinely interested in poetry. But his family was in financial crisis and they hoped he would be a doctor and solve their problem.

Imitation of Spenser" (1814)

"Now Morning from her orient chamber came,
And her first footsteps touch'd a verdant hill;
Crowning its lawny crest with amber flame,
Silv'ring the untainted gushes of its rill;
Which, pure from mossy beds, did down distill,
And after parting beds of simple flowers,
By many streams a little lake did fill,
Which round its marge reflected woven bowers,
And, in its middle space, a sky that never lowers.

---

[9] This poem, "*Imitation of Spenser*", an early work of Keats, was published in 1817 and inspired by reading Edmund Spenser's "*The Fairie Queene*".

*There the king-fisher saw his plumage bright
Vieing with fish of brilliant dye below;
Whose silken fins, and golden scales' light
Cast upward, through the waves, a ruby glow:
There saw the swan his neck of arched snow,
And oar'd himself along with majesty;
Sparkled his jetty eyes; his feet did show
Beneath the waves like Afric's ebony,
And on his back a fay reclined voluptuously..."*

[Excerpts from *'Imitation of Spenser'*]

On the other hand, Keats himself was strongly drawn by his own passion and being inspired by his friends, such as, Charles Cowden Clarke and others, he developed a strong desire

George Keats

of becoming a poet. Faced with the dilemma of choosing between a safe and secure career in medicine and the uncertain career as a poet, he suffered periods of depression. His brother George wrote, "[John] *feared that he should never be a poet, & if he was not he would destroy himself"*.

In 1816, Keats received his apothecary's licence that made him eligible to practise; but before the year was over, by December, he announced that he would be a poet, not a surgeon. Though he decided to be a poet, not a surgeon, Keats continued his work and training at Guy's; but now he began to devote more time to the study of literature, experimenting with verse forms, especially sonnets.

Chapter 2
Keats meets Leigh Hunt: A Turning point in the History of Literature

"There are two worlds: the world we can measure with line and rule, and the world that we feel with our hearts and imagination."

-- Leigh Hunt

Although Keats had already demonstrated an affinity for poetry, (he had written *"Imitation of Spenser"*, his earliest poem we know of, two years before), he had not chosen between his medical career and his literary one up until the end of 1816. The reasons behind that timing might be attributed to a very exciting and stimulating episode in the poet's life, one that it seems marked a turning point not only in his life but also in the history of literature. About this time, Keats through his childhood good friend and former schoolmate Charles Cowden Clarke came to be acquainted with Leigh Hunt, the co-founder of *"The Examiner"*, a leading intellectual journal expounding radical principles, and through him got introduced to a politically involved and artistically devoted circle of artists and thinkers. Hunt was the centre of the Hampstead-based group known as the "*Hunt circle,* that included William Hazlitt and Charles Lamb, ".[10]

---

[10] The '*Hunt circle*' also came to be known as the '*Cockney School*', a derogatory and classist term coined by Blackwood's Edinburgh Magazine in a series of articles criticising the non-aristocratic members of the coterie.

Leigh Hunt

On 9 October, 1816, Keats wrote to his friend Clarke:

> *To C.C. Clarke,*
>
> *Wednesday October 9th*
>
> *"The busy time has now gone by, and I can now devote any time you may mention to the pleasure of seeing Mr. Hunt .... 't will be an Era in my existence ... I am anxious to see the Author of the Sonnet to the Sun, for it is no mean gratification to become acquainted with Men who in their admiration of Poetry do not jumble together Shakespeare and Darwin- I have copied out a sheet or two of verses which I composed some time ago, and find much to blame worst in them that the best part will go into the fire [...]"*

The Clarkes had been supporters of Hunt since the beginning of his newspaper *"The Examiner"*. He and Clarke met during Hunt's stay in gaol, in 1813.[11] Clarke was a culturally involved scholar who cultivated friendships with some of the most well-known names of the period: Charles and Mary Lamb, Shelley, Hunt, Coleridge, the Novello, Godwin and

---

[11] On March 22, 1812 Hunt, in an Examiner editorial and as a part of an ongoing attack on the Prince Regent George, slandered him as a fat "*Adonis*" of 50. As a result, the British government tried both the Hunt brothers, Leigh and John, and sentenced them to two years in prison (February 3, 1813 to February 2, 1815) to pay fines of £500 each. Hunt's was an unusual incarceration. He was permitted to continue editing The Examiner from prison, which he did with little change in the tone of his editorials. During his prison stay Hunt wrote his first long narrative poem, '*The Story of Rimini*'.

Dickens, among others. Thus, he acted as the link between the young Keats and the literary circle of the day that revolved around Hunt.

Keats had been an admirer of Hunt since his senior year at school, when he regularly borrowed *The Examiner* from Clarke. *The Examiner* was a politically independent weekly newspaper, running from 1808 (when Keats was just thirteen) to 1886, edited by Leigh Hunt and printed by his brother John. It was in this newspaper that Hunt established himself as a radical political voice. *The Examiner* published some of the leading radical voices of the time, such as the poets Charles Lamb, Lord Byron or Percy B. Shelley, the painter Benjamin Haydon, or the essayist William Hazlitt. In Hunt's political dissent, Keats found an ideology from which he could draw poetic inspiration. In the words of Clarke, Hunt's paper *"no doubt laid the foundation of his* [Keats's] *love of civil and religious liberty"*. Keats was, therefore, so excited at the prospect of meeting Hunt that he wrote to Clarke that it would be *"an Era in my existence to be acquainted with those who genuinely admire great poetry"*.[12]

Charles Cowden Clarke

---

[12] Through Hunt, Keats almost immediately met Benjamin Robert Haydon (the artist and vocal champion of art) and John Hamilton Reynolds (poet and reviewer). Both began to have some influence on Keats's tastes and ideas; they also further widened Keats's circle of acquaintances particularly in the publishing and art world, of which Keats would have known very little; and both (particularly Haydon) saw that in order to poetically progress, Keats should move from Hunt's influence. In short, the last few months of 1816 and into early 1817 mark, for Keats, a kind of crash course on the Regency London literary and artist culture. In particular, Keats would be thrown face-first in the culture wars of the time, with Hunt's circle generally falling into the progressive, liberal camp.

Although in scholarship Keats's politics tend to be relegated to a second plane, politics played a significant part in his literary outpourings evidence of which is present in his early poems: "*Sonnet. On Peace*", a sonnet he wrote in 1814 calling on the European monarchs to support reform after Napoleon's defeat:

> ***"Sonnet On Peace' (1814)***
>
> *"O Peace! and dost thou with thy presence bless*
> *The dwellings of this war-surrounded Isle;*
> *Soothing with placid brow our late distress,*
> *Making the triple kingdom brightly smile?*
> *Joyful I hail thy presence; and I hail*
> *The sweet companions that await on thee;*
> *Complete my joy let not my first wish fail,*
> *Let the sweet mountain nymph thy favourite be,*
> *With England's happiness proclaim Europa's Liberty.*
> *O Europe! let not sceptred tyrants see*
> *That thou must shelter in thy former state;*
> *Keep thy chains burst, and boldly say thou art free;*
> *Give thy kings law leave not uncurbed the great ;*
> *So with the horrors past thou'lt win thy happier fate!"*
>
> [John Keats, "*Sonnet on Peace*"]

Also, in Keats's "*Lines written on 29 May The Anniversary of the Restoration of Charles the 2nd*", his political identity is clearly discernible:[13]

---

[13] This was written by John Keats in 1814 or 1815. Algernon Sydney, Sir William Russell, and Sir Henry Vane, leaders of the Whig party, were believed to have been involved in the Rye House Plot to execute Charles II and his brother James in 1683. The plot was found out, and they were executed for treason on somewhat flimsy evidence.

> **"Lines written on 29 May/ The Anniversary of the Restoration of Charles the 2nd" (1814 or 1815)**
>
> *"Infatuate Britons, will you still proclaim*
> *His memory, your direst, foulest shame?*
> *Nor patriots revere?*
> *Ah! when I hear each traitorous lying bell,*
> *'Tis gallant Sydney's, Russell's, Vane's sad knell,*
> *That pains my wounded ear."*
>
> [John Keats, *"Lines Written on 29 May, the Anniversary of Charles's Restoration, on Hearing the Bells Ringing"*]

Both the sonnets outlined above of young Keats were very much in line with the style and ideology professed by Hunt. In his biography of John Keats, Robert Gittings argues that, before their acquaintance, Hunt was an inspiration to Keats, a kind of hero, having spent two years in jail (February 3, 1813 to February 2, 1815) for slandering the Prince Regent; he was a role model to Keats to follow:

> *"In search for reassurance, he turned to his intellectual touchstone, The Examiner, and its poet-editor. Here was poetic success which had endured persecution and prison without compromise. Leigh Hunt had done what Keats felt himself failing to do, and kept poetry alive in a workaday world"*. The young poet found in Hunt *"not only* [a] *political exemplar, but* [a] *model for his poetry"*[14].

Prior to their meeting in October, 1816, however, Hunt and Keats's relationship had begun in April that year, when Keats sent his sonnet *"O Solitude"* to his magazine *"The Examiner"* under the initials J.K. and it was published two weeks later.[15] This was the first appearance of Keats's poetry in print; Charles Cowden Clarke was excited and called it his friend's red letter day, first proof that Keats's ambitions were valid. Later that year, Clarke

---

[14] Gittings, Robert: *"John Keats"*, London: Heinemann, 1968.
[15] Mercer Anna: *"On This Day: 9 October 1816, John Keats and Leigh Hunt"*, Bar's Blog, October 9, 2016.

gathered some of Keats's writing and brought it with him to Hampstead, with the intention of showing it to Hunt. Hunt read the manuscripts and reacted

> ***"O Solitude! if I must with thee dwell" (1816)***
>
> *"O Solitude! if I must with thee dwell,*
> *Let it not be among the jumbled heap*
> *Of murky buildings; climb with me the steep,—*
> *Nature's observatory—whence the dell,*
> *Its flowery slopes, its river's crystal swell,*
> *May seem a span; let me thy vigils keep*
> *'Mongst boughs pavillion'd, where the deer's swift leap*
> *Startles the wild bee from the fox-glove bell.*
> *But though I'll gladly trace these scenes with thee,*
> *Yet the sweet converse of an innocent mind,*
> *Whose words are images of thoughts refin'd,*
> *Is my soul's pleasure; and it sure must be*
> *Almost the highest bliss of human-kind,*
> *When to thy haunts two kindred spirits flee."*
>
> [John Keats, '*O Solitude! if I must with thee dwell*']

with great enthusiasm, asking Clarke to bring Keats along on his next visit. In Clarke's own words, their first meeting "*stretched into three morning calls*", and Keats was "*suddenly made a familiar of the household*". Thus began a close relationship that continued until the very last and critical moments of Keats's illness, when the Hunts hosted and took care of a very sick Keats before his departure to Rome, where he breathed his last.

In the summer of 1816, Keats went with Clarke to the seaside town of Margate to write. There he began "*Calidore: A Fragment*" and also initiated the era of his great letter writing. On his return to London, he took lodgings at 8 Dean Street, Southwark and braced himself for further study in order to become a member of the Royal College of Surgeons.

Five months after the first meeting between Keats and Hunt in October 1816, the first volume of Keats's verse, "*Poems*", was published on 3 March

1817, with its dedicatory sonnet to Leigh Hunt. The collection included "*I stood tiptoe*" and "*Sleep and Poetry*", both poems strongly influenced by Hunt. It was a not quite a success, arousing little interest, although Reynolds reviewed it favourably in *The Champion*.[16] Clarke commented that the book "*might have emerged in Timbuctoo*".[17] Keats's publishers, Charles and James Ollier, felt ashamed of the book. Keats immediately changed publishers to Taylor and Hessey on Fleet Street. Unlike Olliers, Keats's new publishers were enthusiastic about his work. Within a month of the publication of Poems they were planning a new Keats volume and had paid him an advance. Hessey became a steady friend to Keats and made the company's rooms available for young writers to meet. Their publishing lists would come to include Coleridge, Hazlitt, Clare, Hogg, Carlyle and Lamb.[18]

At Taylor and Hessey Keats met their Eton-educated lawyer Richard Woodhouse. Woodhouse, who advised the publishers on literary as well as legal matters, was deeply impressed by Poems. Though he noted that Keats could be "*wayward, trembling, easily daunted*", Woodhouse was convinced of Keats's genius, a poet to support as he would become one of the greatest English writers. Soon after they met, the two became close friends and Woodhouse started to collect Keatsiana, documenting as much as he could about Keats's poetry. This archive survives as one of the main sources of information on Keats's poetry. Andrew Motion casts him as Boswell to Keats's Johnson, ceaselessly promoting the writer's work, fighting his corner, spurring his poetry on to greater heights. At the end, Woodhouse would be one of the few people to accompany Keats to Gravesend to embark on his final trip to Rome.[19]

In spite of the bad reviews of "*Poems*", Hunt published in December 1816 in *The Examiner* the essay "*Three Young Poets*" (Shelley, Keats and Reynolds) and the sonnet "*On First Looking into Chapman's Homer*", foreseeing great things to come.[20] He introduced Keats to many prominent men in his circle, including editor of *The Times* Thomas Barnes, writer

---

[16] Gittings, Robert: "*Selected poems and letters of Keats*", London: Heinemann, 1987, pp. 1-3.

[17] Everest, Kelvin: "*Keats, John (1795–1821)*", Oxford Dictionary of National Biography, Oxford University Press, 2004 Online.

[18] Motion, Andrew: "*Keats*". London: Faber, 1997, p.156.

[19] Ibid..

[20] Gittings, Robert: "*John Keats*", London: Heinemann, 1968, p.155.

Charles Lamb, conductor Vincent Novello and poet John Hamilton Reynolds, who would become a close friend. Keats also met William Hazlitt regularly, a powerful literary figure of the day. It was a decisive turning point for Keats, establishing him in the public eye as a figure in what Hunt termed "*a new school of poetry*". At this time Keats wrote to his friend Bailey: "*I am certain of nothing but the holiness of the Heart's affections and the truth of the imagination. What imagination seizes as Beauty must be truth*". This would eventually transmute into the concluding lines of '*Ode on a Grecian Urn*':

"*'Beauty is truth, truth beauty' – that is all*

Ye know on earth, and all ye need to know".

In early December, under the heady influence of his artistic friends, Keats told his guardian Abbey that he had decided to give up medicine in favour of poetry. Abbey, as one would imagine, was thoroughly displeased. Keats had spent a great deal on his medical training and had also made several large loans to friends such as the painter Benjamin Haydon, that he could ill afford. Not only to meet his own financial needs, Keats also lent £700 to his brother George who was also in financial distress. By lending so much, Keats was no longer in a position to repay his own debts.

Having left his training at the hospital, suffering from a succession of colds, and unhappy with living in damp rooms in London, Keats moved with his brothers into rooms at 1 Well Walk in the village of Hampstead in April 1817. Both he and his brother George nursed their brother Tom, who was suffering from tuberculosis. The house was close to the residences of Hunt and others from his circle in Hampstead, as well as to Coleridge's, the illustrious first wave Romantic poet, then living in Highgate. On 11 April 1818, Keats, in a letter to his brother George, wrote that he and Coleridge had taken a long walk on Hampstead Heath, and that they had talked about "*a thousand things,... nightingales, poetry, poetical sensation, metaphysics.*"[21] Around this time Keates was also introduced to Charles Wentworth Dilke, James Rice and Benjamin Bailey.

In June 1818, Keats began a walking tour of Scotland, Ireland and the Lake District with his friend Charles Armitage Brown. Keats's brother George and his wife Georgiana accompanied them as far as Lancaster and

---

[21] Motion, Andrew (1997). "*Keats*". London: Faber, 1997, pp.365-366.

then continued to Liverpool, from where the couple emigrated to America. They lived in Ohio and Louisville, Kentucky until 1841 when George's investments failed. Like Keats's other brother, Tom, they too died penniless and racked by 'consumption'. There was no effective treatment known for the disease until 1921. In July, while on the Isle of Mull, Keats caught a bad cold and "*was too thin and fevered to proceed on the journey*".[22] After his return to south in August, Keats continued to nurse Tom, exposing himself to infection. Some biographers suggest that this is when tuberculosis, their "family disease", first took hold of him. About four months later, Tom died on 1 December 1818.

----

[22] Brown, Charles Armitage: "*Letter of 7 August 1818*", in "The Life of John Keats", ed. London: Oxford University Press, 1937.

Chapter 3
Keats: in love

"Now a soft kiss - Aye, by that kiss, I vow an endless bliss."
-- **John Keats**

In 1818, Keats fell in love.

After the death of his brother, Tom, in December 1818, Keats had moved to his friend Charles Brown's house at Wentworth Place in Hampstead. There he became close to and fell deeply in love with a young neighbour, the 18-year-old Frances (Fanny) Brawne.

Fanny was the daughter of the family which lived next door and Keats initially considered her a 'minx' but could not help falling in love with her. They became engaged in October 1819 but the wedding day never arrived. Stricken by tuberculosis, Keats was advised to seek a warmer climate, and left Britain for Italy in 1820. Alas! for he went there only to die the following year at the age of twenty-five. The two and a half years of their betrothal were among the most poetically productive period for Keats. Their love letters is a timelessly enchanting read in its totality. His final poem to her was simply called: *'To Fanny'*.

"To Fanny" (1819)

>"… *Ah! dearest love, sweet home of all my fears*
>*And hopes and joys and panting miseries,* —
>*To-night, if I may guess, thy beauty wears*
>*A smile of such delight,*
>*As brilliant and as bright,*
>*As when with ravished, aching, vassal eyes,*
>*Lost in a soft amaze,*
>*I gaze, I gaze! …"*

[Excerpts from '*To Fanny*']

Keats and Fanny were in deep love. But she was not his first love.

Isabella Jones: Hush, hush! tread softly! (1818)

> *"Hush, hush! tread softly! hush, hush my dear!*
> *All the house is asleep, but we know very well*
> *That the jealous, the jealous old bald-pate may hear.*
> *Tho' you've padded his night-cap -- O sweet Isabel!*
> *Tho' your feet are more light than a Fairy's feet,*
> *Who dances on bubbles where brooklets meet, --*
> *Hush, hush! soft tiptoe! hush, hush my dear!*
> *For less than a nothing the jealous can hear."*
> *No leaf doth tremble, no ripple is there*
> *On the river, — all's still, and the night's sleepy eye*
> *Closes up, and forgets all its Lethean care,*
> *Charm'd to death by the drone of the humming May-fly;*
> *And the moon, whether prudish or complaisant*
> *Has fled to her bower, well knowing I want:*
> *No light in the dusk, no torch in the gloom,*
> *But my Isabel's eyes, and her lips pulp'd with bloom.*
> *Lift the latch! ah gently! ah tenderly — sweet!*
> *We are dead if that latchet gives one little clink!*
> *Well done — now those lips, and a flowery seat —*
> *The old man may sleep, and the planets may wink;*
> *The shut rose shall dream of our loves and awake*
> *Full-blown, and such warmth for the morning take,*
> *The stock-dove shall hatch his soft twin-eggs and coo,*
> *While I kiss to the melody, aching all through!"*

-- John Keats[23]

---

[23] "As far as I have been able to trace this poem", Forman writes, "it appeared for the first time in the "*Life, Letters, and Literary Remains*" (1848), where it is dated 1818. The statement in the Aldine Edition of 1876 that it was first printed in "*The Literary Pocket-book or Companion for the Lover of Nature and Art*", for 1818, must derive from some misapprehension, as there

Before Keats came to know Fanny, he had, in May 1817, met Isabella Jones, a beautiful, talented and widely read, not of the top flight of society yet financially secure, an enigmatic figure, lady *"in her late 30s"*, while he was on a holiday in the village of Bo Peep near Hastings. He *"frequented her rooms"* in the winter of 1818–19, **Keats** writes in his letters to his brother George, and that he *"warmed with her"* and *"kissed her"*. The trysts may have been a sexual initiation for Keats according to Bate and Robert Gittings.[24] Later, from time to time, he met her in London where she would give him a grouse for his ailing brother.

Jones is believed to have been an inspiration and steward of Keats's writing. The themes of *"The Eve of St. Agnes"* and *"The Eve of St Mark"* may well have been suggested by her; the lyric *Hush, Hush!* ["O sweet Isabel"] was about her. It is also conjectured by some that the first version of "*Bright Star*" may have originally been for her.

In 1821, Jones was one of the first in England to have been informed of Keats's death.[25]

Fanny Brawne

Letters and drafts of poems suggest that Keats first met Fanny Brawne between September and November 1818.[26] It is likely that the 18-year-old Fanny visited the Dilke family at Wentworth Place before she lived there. She was born in the hamlet of West End (now in the district of West Hampstead), on 9 August 1800. Like Keats's grandfather, her grandfather also had a London inn, and both lost several family members to tuberculosis. She shared her first name (Frances) with both Keats's sister and mother, and had a talent for dress-making and languages as well as a natural theatrical inclination. During November 1818 she developed an intimacy with Keats, but it was shadowed by the illness of his brother Tom, whom John was nursing through this period.

---

is no such book. The Pocket-book was started, by Hunt in 1819; and in a copy of the book for that year now in Sir Charles Dilke's possession Keats wrote the Song; but it was not printed in that or in either of the four later Pocket-books which complete the series." [See, Forman, H. Buxton (ed.), "*Poetical Works of John Keats*", Crowell publ., 1895]

[24] Gittings, Robert: "*John Keats*". London: Heinemann, 1968.
[25] Roe, Nicholas: "*John Keats- A New Life*", Yale University Press, 2013.
[26] Ibid., 22, 262.

On 3 April 1819, Fanny and her widowed mother moved into the other half of Dilke's Wentworth Place, and Keats and Fanny were able to see each other every day. Keats began to lend Fanny books, such as Dante's *Inferno*, and they would read together. He gave her the love sonnet "*Bright Star*" (perhaps revised for her) as a declaration of his love. It was a work in progress which he continued until the last months of his life, and the poem came to be associated with their relationship. From this point, there is no further documented mention of Keats's any affair with Isabella Jones.

With Fanny, it was love at first sight that would only grow and seek to defy all worldly limits. In a letter dated 25th July 1819, Keats wrote to her:

> "... I have two luxuries to brood over in my walks, your Loveliness and the hour of my death. ... I hate the world: it batters too much the wings of my self-will, and would I could take a sweet poison from your lips to send me out of it. From no others would I take it... I will imagine you Venus tonight and pray, pray, pray to your star like a Hethen."

Ever since Fanny came in his life, it was the beginning of Keats's most creative period. He wrote, among others, *'The Eve of St Agnes'*, *'La Belle Dame Sans Merci'*, "*Lamia*" and a group of six odes that include, "*Ode on a Grecian Urn*", "*Ode on Indolence*", "*Ode on Melancholy*", "*Ode to a Nightingale*", "*Ode to Psyche*" and *'To Autumn'*. The Odes are Keats's most distinctive poetic achievement and are ranked among the greatest short poems in the English language;

Keats wrote the first five poems, namely, "*Ode on a Grecian Urn*", "*Ode on Indolence*", "*Ode on Melancholy*", "*Ode to a Nightingale*", and "*Ode to Psyche*" in quick succession during the spring, **between March and June 1819**, and he composed "*To Autumn*" in September.

Fanny Brawne

According to Brown, a very close friend of the Keats, a nightingale had built its nest near his house in the spring of 1819.[27] Inspired by the bird's song, Keats composed his *'Ode to a Nightingale'*. It was first published in "*Annals of the Fine Arts*" the following July. In 1882, Swinburne wrote in the *Encyclopaedia Britannica*, "the Ode to a Nightingale" is one of the finest masterpieces of human work in all time and for all ages".

Charles Armitage Brown

---

[27] Brown, Charles Armitage (edited by Dorothy Hyde Bodurtha and W. B. Pope): "*The Life of John Keats*", Oxford University Press, London, 1937.

Keats and Fanny -- they were engaged, but never married. Keats was then a struggling poet; he needed to earn sufficient money before they could get married. Time was not on their side. Because of Keats's terminal illness, the marriage never occurred.

Tuberculosis took hold and Keats was advised by his doctors to move to a warmer climate. In September, 1820 Keats left for Rome knowing he would probably never see Fanny again. After leaving he felt unable to write to her or read her letters, although he did correspond with her mother. None of Fanny's letters to Keats survive.

Five months later, Keats died there in Rome on 23 February 1821, when he was just above 25 years of age.

Chapter 4
1819: Annus Mirabilis

"The only means of strengthening one's intellect is to make up one's mind about nothing, to let the mind be a thoroughfare for all thoughts."

- **John Keats**

Keats's younger brother Tom had died of consumption on December 1, 1818. After Tom's death, Keats moved the same month, namely, in December 1818 to the newly built Wentworth Place, owned by his friend Charles Armitage Brown. The building was originally a pair of semi-detached houses Where Keats lodged with his friend Brown until September 1820 before he left for Rome. It was also on the edge of Hampstead Heath, ten minutes' walk south of his old home in Well Walk. The winter of 1818–19, though a difficult period for the poet, marked the beginning of his annus mirabilis in which he wrote his most mature work. He had been inspired by a series of recent lectures by Hazlitt on English poets and poetic identity and had also met Wordsworth.[28] Keats may have seemed to his friends to be living on comfortable means, but in reality he was borrowing regularly from Abbey and his friends.

---

[28] *"John Keats":* The Oxford Companion to English Literature. Edited by Dinah Birch.

John Keats

At Wentworth Place, Keats composed five of his six great odes possibly between April and May 1819 and, although it is debated in which order they were written, "*Ode to Psyche*" opened the published series. "*Ode on a Grecian Urn*" and "*Ode on Melancholy*" were inspired by sonnet forms and probably written after "*Ode to a Nightingale*". In 1818, Keats's new and progressive publishers Taylor and Hessey published "*Endymion*", which Keats dedicated to Thomas Chatterton, a work that he termed "*a trial of my Powers of Imagination*".[29] It was damned by the critics, a particularly harsh review by John Wilson Croker appeared in the April 1818 edition of the '*Quarterly Review*'. John Gibson Lockhart, writing in '*Blackwood's Magazine*', described '*Endymion*' as "*imperturbable drivelling idiocy*". With biting sarcasm, Lockhart advised,

> "*It is a better and a wiser thing to be a starved apothecary than a starved poet; so back to the shop Mr. John, back to plasters, pills, and ointment boxes.*"

The dismissal was arguably more class-based than literary, sarcastically aimed at upstart young writers deemed uncouth for their lack of education, non-formal rhyming and "*low diction*" --- directed particularly, at those who had not attended Eton, Harrow or Oxbridge and were not from the upper classes.[30]

In 1819, Keats wrote "*The Eve of St. Agnes*", "*La Belle Dame sans Merci*", "*Hyperion*", "*Lamia*" and a play, "*Otho the Great*", written by him in collaboration with his friend Charles Brown, who planned its construction. The play was critically damned and not performed until 1950.[31] The poems "*Fancy*" and "*Bards of passion and of mirth*" were inspired by the garden of Wentworth Place. In September, at a time when he was very short of money and in despair was considering taking up journalism or a post as a ship's surgeon, he approached his publishers with a new book of poems.[32] They

---

[29] Everest, Kelvin: "*Keats, John (1795–1821)*", Oxford Dictionary of National Biography, Oxford University Press, 2004 Online.

[30] Motion, Andrew: "*Keats*". London: Faber, 1997, pp. 204-205.

[31] Watts, Cedric Thomas: "*A preface to Keats*", Longman, University of Michigan, 1985, p. 90.

[32] Everest, Kelvin: "*Keats, John (1795–1821)*", Oxford Dictionary of National Biography, Oxford University Press, 2004 Online.

were, however, unimpressed with the collection, finding the presented versions of "*Lamia*" confusing, and describing "*St Agnes*" as having a "*sense of pettish disgust*" and "*a 'Don Juan' style of mingling up sentiment and sneering*" concluding it was "*a poem unfit for ladies*" [33] The poems were eventually published as "*Lamia, Isabella, The Eve of St. Agnes, and Other Poems*", during Keats's lifetime in July 1820. It received greater acclaim than had *Endymion* or *Poems*, finding favourable notices in both *The Examiner* and *Edinburgh Review*, and came to be recognised as one of the most important poetic works ever published.[34]

Wentworth Place now houses a writer's house museum, known as "*Keats House museum*".

Keats House museum

---

[33] Gittings, Robert: "*John Keats*". London: Heinemann, 1968, p. 504.
[34] Everest, Kelvin: "*Keats, John (1795–1821)*", Oxford Dictionary of National Biography, Oxford University Press, 2004 Online.

Chapter 5
December 20, 1819: Keats hesitates on the threshold of a career in business

"Where are the songs of Spring? Aye, where are they?
Think not of them; thou has thy music too."

-- **John Keats**

Keats lived in a poetic world. He dreamt poetry. But, interestingly, for a change as one can see in the following letter, for at least one brief moment in 1819, the year he was at the peak of creative spree, the young (and certainly sad and disgusted) Keats seems to have seriously considered the possibility of quitting poetry for the business of tea brokerage.

The year 1819 was in many ways a critical year in Keats's life. Earlier he had completed his study of medicine and worked in a hospital before publishing his first book of poems in 1817. The following year he published '*Endymion*' and was subjected to the **scandalous and vitriolic criticisms** of the mighty critics on '*Blackwood's Edinburgh Magazine*' and to the savage and condescending abuse of the '*Quarterly Review*'. To worsen matters, Keats's health deteriorated, his slender funds began to run out; there were also troubles on his family front – his brother George departed for America, and his own love affair with Fanny Brawne went through the most desperate anguish of jealousy and uncertainty. Ironically, in spite of so many problems, throughout the year 1819, he was on a creative spree having written most of his best works during this period. But the second great volume of his poetry "*Lamia, Isabella, the Eve of St Agnes and Other Poems*" was yet to be published and as such he was at that time quite an unknown poet whose only published work till then had been subject to savage criticism by an influential section of the critics. Faced with so many problems, the young Keats began to feel the pinch of acute monetary crisis and was looking for avenues to supplement his income.

In the letter that follows, Keats explains to his sister Fanny that his guardian Mr. Abbey, who was in the tea business, had just given him an opportunity to enter upon a career as a 'tea broker' He understands that it "*might be executed with little trouble and good profit*", but still he is not excited and in the end he feels it will not suit him and decides to give it up. In the letter, he further discusses his "*literary hopes*" and refers to "*some poems*" he is "*preparing*":

"...Tea Brokerage ... will not suit me"

"*Wentworth Place, Monday, Morn.*
[December 20, 1819]

MY DEAR FANNY,

When I saw you last, you ask'd me whether you should see me again before Christmas. You should have seen me if I had been quite well. I have not, though not unwell enough to have prevented me --- not indeed at all ---- but fearful le[s]t the weather should affect my throat which on exertion or cold continually threaten me. By the advice of my Doctor, I have had a wa[r]m great Coat made and have ordered some thick shoes ---- so furnish'd I shall be with you if it holds a little fine before the Christmas day.

I have been very busy since I saw you especially the last Week and shall be for some time, in preparing some Poems to come out in the Spring ... My hopes of success in the literary world now better than ever. Mr. Abbey, on my calling of him lately, appeared anxious that I should apply myself to something else – He mentioned Tea Brokerage. I supposed he might perhaps mean to give me the Brokerage of his concern, which might be executed with little trouble and good profit; and therefore said I have no objection to it especially as it the same time it occur[r]ed to me that I might make over the business to George ----- I questioned him about it a few days after. His mind takes odd turns. When I became a Sutor, he became coy. He did not seem so much inclined to serve me. He described what I should have to do in the progress of the business. It will not suit me. I have given it up [...]

I am, ever, my dear Sister
Yours affectionately
John Keats"

Shortly after he wrote this letter, Keats was to learn, in his own words, *"circumstances are like Clouds, continually gathering and bursting."* In a subsequent letter, he went on to say, *"While we are laughing, the seed of some trouble is put into the wide, arable land of events ... While we are laughing, it sprouts, it grows and suddenly bears a poison fruit we must pluck."* It was so true for Keats and one wonders how he knew it so well; for four years were too little a room into which he had to crowd all the things he had to say. He published his first book of poems at the age of 21, and breathed his last when he was just over 25.[35]

---

[35] Schuster, M. Lincoln: *"The World's Great Letters"*, Simon & Schuster, New York, 1940, pp.245-247.

Chapter 6
Keats: Early Works

"What the imagination seizes as beauty must be truth."

- John Keats

John Keats took his place among the great English poets in the narrow space of six years. He was twenty when he first had a poem published in 1816, twenty-one when the first volume of his poetry appeared, and twenty-two when the second followed. In the same year his work was ferociously attacked in the press and his young brother Tom died of tuberculosis; and at the same time he fell in love with Fanny Brawne, with no prospect of marriage. His health was never good. Yet an *annus mirabilis* followed, in the course of which he wrote a series of master works that included *"The Eve of St Agnes"*, '*La Belle Dame sans Merci*' '*Lamia'*, the long fragment of '*Hyperion'* and the great odes. All were published in July 1820, in his third and last volume.

1816: "On First Looking into Chapman's Homer"

In October 1816, Keats wrote the sonnet *"On First Looking into Chapman's Homer"*, inspired by George Chapman's classic 17th-century translation of the '*Iliad'* and the '*Odyssey'*. The sonnet was written in the early hours of one morning after he had spent the entire night reading a copy of George Chapman's 1616 translation of Homer's Iliad and Odyssey. Keats returned home from Clerkenwell to Dean Street, where he quickly wrote out a draft of the poem, which he then sent back to Clerkenwell, to his friend Charles Cowden Clarke, with whom he had sat up all night, excitedly reading.

> **"On First Looking into Chapman's Homer"** (1816)
>
> *Much have I travell'd in the realms of gold,*
> *And many goodly states and kingdoms seen;*
> *Round many western islands have I been*
> *Which bards in fealty to Apollo hold.*
> *Oft of one wide expanse had I been told*
> *That deep-brow'd Homer ruled as his demesne;*
> *Yet did I never breathe its pure serene*
> *Till I heard Chapman speak out loud and bold:*
> *Then felt I like some watcher of the skies*
> *When a new planet swims into his ken;*
> *Or like stout Cortez when with eagle eyes*
> *He star'd at the Pacific—and all his men*
> *\Look'd at each other with a wild surmise—*
> *Silent, upon a peak in Darien.*

Keats's sonnet *"On First Looking into Chapman's Homer"* was first published in Hunt's *'The Examiner'*, along with a short essay by Hunt that named Keats, Percy B. Shelley, and John Hamilton Reynolds as *"Young Poets of a new school of poetry"* having promises to restore the same love of Nature, which formerly rendered us real poets, and not merely versifying wits, and bead-rollers of couplets. Hunt was, however, mildly condescending in his brief discussion of the three poets as it was implicit in his comments that these three were, in effect, his poetic wards. Referring to Keats's poem, Hunt, rather teacherly, pointed to a little vagueness in Keats's phrasing, and also picked out one incorrect rhyme, but the poem was judged as excellent; and having seen other poems by Keats, Hunt told his readers that they were surprising in the truth of their ambition, and ardent grappling with Nature. One can imagine how being written about by Hunt in a journal that Keats greatly esteemed must have significantly reinforced his poetic ambitions. How could a young, unknown poet not have been very excited?

For his part, Hunt marked the occasion with his own sonnet to Keats, one which pictured Keats with a flowering laurel on his brow. Hunt, too, flattered himself that Keats saw him as possessing senses that discerningly perceive the loveliness of things. Hunt's sonnet was a little self-serving, and might be translated as, '*Follow me Keats, and you too will be able to poetically see into all things—including nature, human nature, and even female form . . .*'

As for the Keats's sonnet itself, what is immediately discernible is the memorable phrasing that captures the drama of imaginative and inspirational discovery. The poem beautifully displays the aspirations of a young, awestruck poet-in-progress—someone on the margins looking with covetous awe at the qualities and achievement of epic poetry. The poem ends with Cortez/Keats[36] looking out toward future with wonder, uncertainty, intimidation, and possible direction, which exactly captures his position as a poet at this point in his poetic progress. The poem is a decent allegory of poetic potential.

Keats's First Book: 'Poems' (1817)

Keats's first book, "*Poems*", was published on 3 March 1817 by Charles and James Ollier, who were already publishing Shelley. The first of a mere three lifetime publications, it is a work of mainly youthful promise. Keats had appeared for the first time in print less than a year earlier, with a poem in the radical weekly "*The Examiner*" on 5 May 1816. The 1817 '*Poems*' attracted a few good reviews, but these were followed by the first of several harsh attacks by the influential Blackwood's Magazine, mainly by critics who resented Keats's avowed kinship with Leigh Hunt who was thoroughly despised by them.

The best-known poem in Keats's first book, "*Poems*", is the sonnet "*On first looking into Chapman's Homer*" (published a year ago in '*The Examiner*' edited by Leigh Hunt), "*by common consent one of its masterpieces in this form, having a close unsurpassed for the combined qualities of serenity and concentration*" (Colvin)[37], and described by Oxford

---

[36] Keats happens to make a historical error in the poem. The explorer who stood on a peak to gaze upon the Pacific (in December 1513) was in fact Balboa, not Cortez. Some too-ingenious criticism seek to posit that Keats's mistake is intentional; but common sense, and given the early stage of Keats's poetic career, makes this suggestion rather tendentious. Keats simply gets his explorers mixed up, and none of Keats's exceedingly well-read friends noticed the error either.

[37] Colvin, Sydney: "*Keats*", Palala Press, 24 February 2018

Dictionary of National Biography (ODNB) as *"an astonishing achievement, with a confident formal assurance and metaphoric complexity which make it one of the finest English sonnets"*. As Hunt generously acknowledged, it *"completely announced the new poet taking possession"*.

Endymion (1818)

> *"A thing of beauty is a joy for ever:*
> *Its loveliness increases; it will never*
> *Pass into nothingness; ..."*
>
> **[John Keats, *"Endymion"*]**

In 1817 Keats left London briefly for a trip to the Isle of Wight and Canterbury and began work on '*Endymion*', a four-thousand-line long poem based on the Greek legend of love of the moon goddess for Endymion, a shepherd. On his return to London, he moved into lodgings in Hampstead with his brothers. On November 28, 1818, Keats completed *"Endymion",*. Keats transformed the tale into the Romantic theme of an ideal love. In his wanderings, Endymion is guilty of an apparent infidelity to his visionary moon goddess as he falls in love with an earthly maiden to whom he is attracted by human sympathy. But in the end the goddess and the earthly maiden turn out to be one and the same.

Written in rhyming couplets in iambic pentameter (also known as heroic couplets)[38], *Endymion* was first published in 1818 by Taylor and Hessey of Fleet Street in London. Keats dedicated this poem to the late poet Thomas Chatterton. The poem begins with the line "*A thing of beauty is a joy for ever*".

---

[38] In the English language, iambic pentameter is a type of verse that alternates short syllables and long syllables to create a rhythm. In English writing, rhythm is measured by groups of syllables called "feet." Iambic pentameter uses a type of foot called an "iamb," which is a short, unstressed syllable followed by a longer, stressed syllable. A line written in iambic pentameter contains five iambic feet—hence, pentameter.

Each line written in iambic pentameter, therefore, has five sets of two beats, the first is unstressed and the second is stressed. E.g. "*Shall I compare thee to a summer's day?*" where the bold beats are stressed, and the underlined beats are unstressed.

"Endymion" (1818)

"A thing of beauty is a joy for ever:
Its loveliness increases; it will never
Pass into nothingness; but still will keep
A bower quiet for us, and a sleep
Full of sweet dreams, and health, and quiet breathing.
Therefore, on every morrow, are we wreathing
A flowery band to bind us to the earth,
Spite of despondence, of the inhuman dearth
Of noble natures, of the gloomy days,
Of all the unhealthy and o'er-darkened ways
Made for our searching: yes, in spite of all,
Some shape of beauty moves away the pall
From our dark spirits. Such the sun, the moon,
Trees old and young, sprouting a shady boon
For simple sheep; and such are daffodils
With the green world they live in; and clear rills
That for themselves a cooling covert make
'Gainst the hot season; the mid forest brake,
Rich with a sprinkling of fair musk-rose blooms:
And such too is the grandeur of the dooms
We have imagined for the mighty dead;
All lovely tales that we have heard or read:
An endless fountain of immortal drink,
Pouring unto us from the heaven's brink.. ...."

[Excerpts from '*Endymion*', Book I]

In a letter to his brother George, Keats described the poem as "*a text, a trial of my Powers of Imagination and chiefly of my invention ... by which I must make 4000 lines of one bare circumstance and fill them with poetry*". As he notes in the preface, he considered it an apprentice work. This '*circumstance'* was the story of Greek Shepherd Endymion for which Keats drew on classical dictionaries by Tooke and Lemprière for information; the latter explains that

> "*The fable ... arises from* [Endymion's] *knowledge of astronomy, and as he passed the night on some high mountain, to observe the moon, it has been reported that he was courted by the moon.*"

Other literary accounts of the myth include those by John Lyly (1588) and Michael Drayton (1595).

Keats began the poem in 1817, and revised its four books in 1818 on the basis of a monthly cycle, forwarding each corrected book to his publisher at the full moon.

Perhaps because of its presumptions to the educated territory of classical myth, the work was savagely attacked by a section of the press. Perhaps because of its presumptions to the educated territory of classical myth, it was savagely attacked by a section of the press. Keats himself was also not too happy with its somewhat diffuse style, but he did not regret writing it as he likened the process to leaping into the ocean to become more acquainted with his surroundings. In a poem to J. A. Hessey, he expressed that "*I was never afraid of failure; for I would sooner fail than not be among the greatest.*" Keats, however, did express regret in its publishing, saying "*it is not without a feeling of regret that I make* [Endymion] *public.*"

Keats: A victim of his critics

> "*it is a better and a wiser thing to be a starved apothecary than a starved poet; so back to the shop, Mr John, back to the 'plasters, pills, and ointment boxes.*"
>
> **-- John Gibson Lockhart, critic, 'Blackwood's Magazine' in a review of Keats's 'Endymion'**

"*Endymion*" was a masterpiece. On reading it, Shelly complimented Keats saying "*...you are capable of the greatest things...* " But when it was published, Keats was subjected to the full fury of the mighty critics on '*Blackwood's Edinburgh Magazine*' and to the savage and condescending abuse of the '*Quarterly Review*'.

In *'Blackwood's Magazine'*, **John Gibson Lockhart**, the writer, critic and son-in-law of Sir Walter Scott, 1st Baronet, the famous Scottish historical novelist, poet and playwright, hiding behind the initial "Z", criticised Keats's work as *'mawkish'* and *'bad-mannered'*, as the work of an upstart *"vulgar Cockney poetaster"*, due to what Lockhart considered to be Keats's relative lack of literary education. In a harsh review of *'Endymion'*, he ridiculed Keats's literary ambitions saying,[39]

> *"John Keats's friends, we understand, destined him to the career of medicine, and he was bound apprentice to a worthy apothecary in town. It is a better and wiser thing to be a starved apothecary than a starved poet; so back to the shop, Mr John, back to 'plasters, pills, and ointment boxes'. But for heaven's sake be a little more sparing of extenuatives and soporifics in your practice than you have been in your poetry."*

The *'Quarterly Review'* critic, **John Wilson Croker,** who was known for his aversion for the younger school of poets, also savagely criticised Keats's *"Endymion"* as consisting of *"the most incongruous ideas in the most uncouth language".*

The scandalous, vitriolic critiques not only demoralised Keats, it also adversely affected his health and is believed to have hastened his death.[40]

Leigh Hunt blamed Keats's death on the *Quarterly Review*'s scathing attack of *"Endymion".* Grief over the untimely death of Keats as well as intense indignation at the unjust cruelty of the critics toward the poetry of his friend inspired Shelley to write *'Adonais'* the following month at Pisa. Lord Byron, on the other hand, who had a rivalrous relation with Keats, in a shameful display of insensitivity, quipped in his narrative poem *"Don Juan":*

---

[39] *"Don't give up the day job, Keats: how the poetic greats were snubbed"*, 23 August, 2021. https://shorturl.at/prMZ6

[40] Not all critics, however, disliked Keats's work in *'Endymion'*. According to the noted English critic Henry Morley, "*The song of Endymion throbs throughout with a noble poet's sense of all that his art means for him. What mechanical defects there are in it may even serve to quicken our sense of the youth and freshness of this voice of aspiration."*

Later critics such as Andrew Motion, who was Poet Laureate from 1999 to 2009, have also argued that the youthful '*waywardness*' of '*Endymion*' is '*its greatest triumph*', and its opening lines would become some of the most famous in the English language.

"'Tis strange the mind, that very fiery particle
Should let itself be snuffed out by an article."

[Byron, Don Juan, canto 11, stanza 60]

Lord George Gordon Byron

Keats never complained. But in the silence of the graveyard in Rome, the inscription on his tombstone bares it all.[41]

---

[41] See, The Prologue: "His Last Words":
The inscription on the headstone of Keats' tomb reads:
"*This Grave contains all that was Mortal, of a YOUNG ENGLISH POET,*
Who on his Death Bed, in the Bitterness of his Heart at the Malicious Power of his Enemies,
Desired these Words to be engraven on his Tomb Stone
"*Here lies One*
Whose Name was writ in Water"
February 24, 1821"
Keats desired only the phrase "*Here lies one whose name was writ in water*" inscribed on his tombstone. Just this phrase; he did not even want his name to appear on his tombstone; merely this line, for he was so embittered with life by the time his death was near.
The rest of the inscription was added by his friends Severn and Charles Brown. Both were grief-stricken and resentful of the savage critical treatment of Keats's poetry, particularly by the critics of '*Blackwood's Magazine*' and the '*Quarterly Review*'.

Chapter 7
Keats: Masterpieces

"I have no trust whatever on Poetry. ... The marvel is to me how people read so much of it."

-- John Keats

Isabella, or the Pot of Basil (1817-18)

"O cruelty, To steal my Basil- pot away from me!"

[John Keats, *"Isabella, or the Pot of Basil"*]

Soon after the completion of *Endymion*, Keats wrote a narrative poem "*Isabella, or the Pot of Basil*" in 1818, an adaptation of the story of the '*Pot of Basil*' in Giovanni Boccaccio's "*Decameron*" and again he was dissatisfied with his work.

The poem "*Isabella, or the Pot of Basil*" tells the tale of a young woman whose family intends to marry her to "*a high noble and his olive trees*", but who falls for Lorenzo, one of her brothers' employees. When the brothers learn of this they murder Lorenzo and bury his body. His ghost informs Isabella in a dream. She exhumes the body and buries the head in a pot of basil which she tends obsessively, while pining for her love. Her obsessive tending of the pot of basil arouses the suspicions of her brothers'. One day they steal away the pot and Isabella is left alone to die in pain, mourning the death of her true love.

The poem explores themes of love, death, and the power of emotions. It portrays the intense and tragic nature of love, as well as the societal constraints that can lead to such tragedy. Keats's beautiful and melancholic verses capture the emotional depth of Isabella's love and her profound grief over her lost lover.

"*Isabella, or the Pot of Basil*" (1817-1818)

"FAIR Isabel, poor simple Isabel!
Lorenzo, a young palmer in Love's eye!
They could not in the self-same mansion dwell
Without some stir of heart, some malady;
They could not sit at meals but feel how well
It soothed each to be the other by;
They could not, sure, beneath the same roof sleep
But to each other dream, and nightly weep.
With every morn their love grew tenderer,
With every eve deeper and tenderer still;
He might not in house, field, or garden stir,
But her full shape would all his seeing fill;
And his continual voice was pleasanter
To her, than noise of trees or hidden rill;
Her lute-string gave an echo of his name,
She spoilt her half-done broidery with the same. ..."

[Excerpts from "*Isabella, or the Pot of Basil*"]

Published in 1820 along with some others, "*Isabella*," which Keats himself called "*a weak-sided poem*," contains some of the emotional weaknesses of '*Endymion*'. The poem, however, was quite popular with Pre-Raphaelite painters, who illustrated several episodes from it, notably, '*Isabella and the Pot of Basil*' by William Holman Hunt (1868), '*Isabella and the Pot of Basil*' by John William Waterhouse (1907) and '*Isabella*' (also known as '*Lorenzo and Isabella*') by John Everett Millais (1848-49). Later, John White Alexander depicted the poem in his 1897 '*Isabella and the Pot of Basil*', currently held at the Museum of Fine Arts, Boston. Frank Bridge also wrote a symphonic poem of the same name in 1907.

John William Waterhouse (1849-1917)
Isabella and the Pot of Basil, 1907

The Eve of St. Agnes (1819)

"The Eve of St. Agnes"

"St. Agnes' Eve—Ah, bitter chill it was!
The owl, for all his feathers, was a-cold;
The hare limp'd trembling through the frozen grass,
And silent was the flock in woolly fold:
Numb were the Beadsman's fingers, while he told
His rosary, and while his frosted breath,
Like pious incense from a censer old,
Seem'd taking flight for heaven, without a death,
Past the sweet Virgin's picture, while his prayer he saith."
His prayer he saith, this patient, holy man;
Then takes his lamp, and riseth from his knees,
And back returneth, meagre, barefoot, wan,
Along the chapel aisle by slow degrees:

> *The sculptur'd dead, on each side, seem to freeze,*
> *Emprison'd in black, purgatorial rails:*
> *Knights, ladies, praying in dumb orat'ries,*
> *He passeth by; and his weak spirit fails*
> *To think how they may ache in icy hoods and mails.*
>
> [Excerpts from *"The Eve of Saint Agnes"*]

The poem *"Isabella, or the Pot of Basil"* was a precursor to *"The Eve of St. Agnes"*, both set in the Middle Ages and relate to passionate and dangerous romance. *"The Eve of St. Agnes"*, represents an idyllic view of love, and was written in the dead of the winter of 1819 in the first flush of his tryst with Brawne, his lady love. 1819 was basically "The Year" for Keats because it was the year he wrote all but one of the Odes, his most famous poems. *"The Eve of St. Agnes"* is the first thing he wrote that year. It was first published in 1820 along with '*La Belle Dame*'. '*Isabella*' and the five famous Odes, and '*Lamia*' and '*Hyperion*'. It is considered to be one of the finest books of poems ever given to the world.

The title of the poem comes from the day (or evening) before the feast[42] of Saint Agnes (or St. Agnes's Eve). St. Agnes, the patron saint of virgins, died a martyr in 4th century Rome. The eve falls on 20 January; the feast day on the 21st. The divinations referred to by Keats in this poem are referred to by John Aubrey in his *Miscellanies* (1696) as being associated with St. Agnes's night.

The poem is based on the folk belief that a girl could see her future husband in a dream if she performed certain rites on the eve of St. Agnes, like, transferring pins one by one from a pincushion to a sleeve while reciting the Lord's Prayer, walking backwards upstairs to bed without any supper. Another tradition was to eat a portion of dumb cake[43] before retiring to bed, hoping to dream of her future love:

"St Agnes, that's to lovers kind

---

[42] The calendar of saints is the traditional Christian method of organizing a liturgical year by associating each day with one or more saints and referring to the day as the feast day or feast of said saint. The word "feast" in this context does not mean "a large meal, ", but instead "an annual religious celebration, a day dedicated to a particular saint".

[43] A salty confection prepared with friends in total silence.

Come ease the trouble of my mind"[44]

Then the future husband would appear in her dream.

In Scotland, girls would meet in a field of crops at midnight, throw grain on to the soil and pray:

"Agnes sweet, and Agnes fair,

Hither, hither, now repair;

Bonny Agnes, let me see

The lad who is to marry me."

The Legend of St. Agnes

But who was St Agnes?

Agnes was a beautiful young Christian girl of good family who lived in Rome in the early 4th century. The son of a Roman prefect wanted to marry her but she refused him, as she had decided to devote herself to religious purity.

Angered by her refusal, the snubbed suitor denounced her to the authorities as a Christian. Agnes's punishment was to be thrown into a public brothel. She was, however, somehow spared this terrible ordeal. According to one legend, all the men who attempted to rape her were immediately struck blind or paralyzed. In another, her virginity was preserved by thunder and lightning from Heaven.

Saint Agnes - painted by Massimo Stanzione[45]

---

[44] Castelow, Ellen: "Eve of St. Agnes", Historic UK.
[45] 'Saint Agnes' is an oil-on-canvas painting executed ca. 1635–1640 by the Italian Baroque painter Massimo Stanzione. It is now in the National Art Museum of Catalonia. [Source: Wikipedia]

Condemned as a witch and sentenced to be burnt to death, the young Agnes was then tied to the stake but the wood would not burn; so one of the guards beheaded her with his sword. Agnes was only 12 or 13 years old when she died on 21st January. When her parents visited her tomb eight days later, they were met by a chorus of angels, including Agnes with a white lamb, a symbol of purity, by her side.[46]

Agnes (c. 291 – c. 304), the virgin martyr, was venerated as a saint in the Catholic Church, Oriental Orthodox Church and the Eastern Orthodox Church, as well as the Anglican Communion and Lutheran Churches. She is, among other patronages, a patron saint of girls, chastity, virgins, victims of sex abuse and gardeners.

The Plot

The poem '*The Eve of St Agnes*' tells the story of Madeline and her lover Porphyro. As mentioned earlier, Keats, in the poem, refers to the tradition of girls hoping to dream of their future lovers on the Eve of St Agnes.

The poem begins with an elderly beadsman[47] saying his prayers on a bitterly chill night, in the chapel of the ancestral home of Madeline's family, where a loud party has begun. It is January 20, the eve of the Feast of St. Agnes, when Madeline, the daughter of the lord of the castle, is anxiously looking forward to midnight, for she has been assured by "*old dames*" that, if she performs certain rites such as going supperless to bed, she will have a magical vision of her lover at midnight in her dreams. Madeline pines for the love of Porphyro, a young nobleman, but Madeline's family regards him as a sworn enemy whom they are eager to kill on sight.

Later that night, Porphyro, who is also in love with Madeline, makes his way to the castle at a considerable risk to his life. The presence of many guests in the castle helps make it convenient for Porphyro to escape notice. Inside the castle, he seeks out Madeline's old nurse Angela, an elderly woman, who is friendly to him and his family, Somehow he is able to meet Angela who, after a lot of persuasion, agrees to help him. Angela tells Porphyro of Madeline's quaint superstition that she would be able to see her future husband in her dream tonight on the eve of St. Agnes. At once the idea

---

[46] Castelow, Ellen: "Eve of St. Agnes", Historic UK.
[47] A person who prays for another as a duty, especially when paid. [See, Dictionary.com]

of making Madeline's belief become reality by his presence in her bedroom at midnight flashes into Porphyro's mind. With the help of Angela, he enters Madeline's chamber where he hides in a closet. All he wishes is to secretly gaze on the sleeping beauty of Madeline, with the fairies who bring dreams walking over her blankets, and magic keeping her asleep.

After a while. Madeline enters her chamber with her mind filled with the thought of the wonderful vision she will soon have, goes to bed and falls asleep. Porphyro creeps forth as she sleeps; half-asleep Madeline wakes and sees before her the same man she has seen in her dream and, thinking Porphyro part of it, receives him into her bed. Waking in full and realising her mistake, she tells Porphyro she cannot hate him for his deception since her heart is so much in his, but that if he goes now he would leave behind,

"A dove forlorn and lost

With sick unpruned wing".

Porphyro declares his love for Madeline, promises her a home with him over the southern moors, and urges her to leave the castle with him.

"Awake! arise! my love, and fearless be,

For o'er the southern moors I have a home for thee."

The two then flee from the castle, passing unconscious, drunken revellers and go out into the storm.

That night the "*Baron*" (Madeline's father) and all his warrior-guests have bad dreams of witches and demons, while Angela dies and the beadsman too as he sleeps "*among his ashes cold*".

Critique

The Eve of St. Agnes" by John Keats is widely regarded as one of his masterpieces and a significant contribution to Romantic literature. The poem showcases Keats's exceptional ability to create vivid imagery, evoke emotions, and explore complex themes.

Based on account of an idealized love between two beautiful and heroic characters, the '*Eve of St. Agnes*' is a poem of epic length written in Spenserian, nine-line style. The first eight lines of each stanza is written in iambic pentameter with the last, known as an "alexandrine" written in iambic hexameter. The first eight lines have five beats per line while the last has six.

Some critics view the poem as Keats's celebration of his first and only experience of romance. "*The Eve of St. Agnes*" was, in fact, considered somewhat scandalous when it was first published, mainly on account of the apparent sensuality of Madeline and Porphyro's encounter in Madeline's chamber.

The poem describes a passionate, warm scene, but opens and closes with an air of coldness. Coldness seems to stand for cautiousness, religiosity, and age, while warmth represents youthful passion and the pursuit of pleasure. The first two stanzas of the poem depict a "b*eadsman*" praying the rosary on a bitterly cold night, acting out penance for sins not explicitly stated; "*the joys of all his life were said and sung*". He cuts a desolate figure, and it is not clear whether Keats intends him as an object of respect or ridicule. In any case, the beadsman has clearly renounced all earthly pleasures. The "*argent revelry*" of courtly people, who are decked out in "*rich array*" provides a sharp contrast. The Baron's guests at the party all act as foils for the steadfast beadsman, and appear to be concerned with ephemeral matters such as wealth, music, and dance. They are but "*shadows haunting fairily*"

From the standpoint of romanticism, it is arguably the loveliest "*English pure romance poem of its time*" with a medieval background, says one critic. In this poem, Keats has woven the motive of a love-passion between the son and daughter of two hostile families reminding us of Romeo and Juliet. As a poet of medievalism, Keats concentrates upon the passion rather than the adventure of the period. He does not make Porphyro fight with his enemies but dwells upon his passion for Madeline. Porphyro came with his "*heart on fire*" for her. Madeline's word to Porphyro are also full of passion:

"*Oh leave me not in this eternal woe,*

For if thou diest, my love, I know not where to go."

"*The Eve of St. Agnes,*" says English poet, playwright, and critic John Drinkwater, "*must be reckoned, on the whole, the most splendid of Keats's poems*". Keats takes in the poem the simple, almost thread-bare theme of the love of an adventurous youth for the daughter of a hostile house, "*a story wherein something of Romeo and Juliet is mixed with something of young Lochinvar"* - and brings it very cleverly and skilfully into association with the old popular belief as to the way a maiden might, on the anniversary of St. Agnes's Eve, win sight of her lover in a dream.

MacCracken is of the view that the substance of the story is derived from a tale by Boccaccio, *"Keats's narrative is truly like a magically refined and enriched quintessence distilled from the correspondence chapter in Boccaccio's tale."*[48]

"*The Eve of St. Agnes*", according to critics, is marked by a rich sensuousness which is also a romantic trait. The description of the feast spread by Porphyro appeals to our senses of smell, sight and taste. The picture of the window panes with their splendid dyes is perfect in its beauty of colour and delights our sense of sight. Our sense of sight is also gratified when the poet refers to the moon throwing its light on Madeline's fair breast.

The music of the poem and its phrases of rare beauty also lend it a romantic quality. Keats, according to the critics, has handled the Spenserian stanza with great finesse while he gives us intoxicating phrases, such as, "*warmed jewels*" which Madeline takes off -- jewels warmed by her body. Such expressions are remarkable departure from the stale, artificial and bombastic diction of the 18th century poetry. These phrases make the poem ornate --- as they decorate and beautify it beyond measure.

---

[48] "The Eve of St. Agnes: Poem by John Keats – Analysis", Literature Analysis. https://t.ly/u2PYM

Chapter 8
Keats: More Masterpieces I

"I have given up Hyperion, there were too many Miltonic inversions in it—Miltonic verse cannot be written because it is an artist's humour and I wish to give myself up to other sensations. English ought to be kept up."

-- John Keats

Hyperion (1819)

"Deep in the shady sadness of a vale
Far sunken from the healthy breath of morn,
Far from the fiery noon, and eve's one star,
Sat gray-hair'd Saturn, quiet as a stone,
Still as the silence round about his lair;...
Forest on forest hung about his head
Like cloud on cloud. No stir of air was there,
Not so much life as on a summer's day
Robs not one light seed from the feather'd grass,
But where the dead leaf fell, there did it rest.
A stream went voiceless by, still deadened more
By reason of his fallen divinity
Spreading a shade: the Naiad 'mid her reeds
Press'd her cold finger closer to her lips...."

[Excerpts from "*Hyperion*" *(1819)*]

"*Hyperion*" is an abandoned epic poem of Keats, in two versions. He wrote it from late 1818 until the spring of 1819, when he gave it up as he felt it was having "*too many Miltonic inversions*[49]. The poem stops abruptly in the middle of the third book, with close to 900 lines having been completed. This unfinished first version was published in 1820. This was when he was also nursing his younger brother Tom, who died on 1 December, 1818 of tuberculosis

Keats picked up the incomplete work once again in late 1819 in "*The Fall of Hyperion: A Dream*", a revised edition of his earlier work with a long prologue, which was also left unfinished and was published posthumously in 1856. He attempted to recast the epic by framing it with a personal quest to find truth and understanding. The poem is the last of Keats's many attempts to reconcile his perceived conflict between mortal decay and absolute value. That same autumn (1819) Keats contracted tuberculosis, and by the following February he felt that death was already upon him, referring to the present as his "*posthumous existence.*"

Plot

In Hyperion, the epic subject is the supersession of the earlier Greek gods, the Titans, by the later Olympian gods. In this poem, Keats consciously attempts to emulate the epic loftiness of John Milton's "*Paradise Lost*". The poem narrates the story of Hyperion, the sun god of the Titans, who were supplanted by the Olympians. The poem opens with the Titans already fallen, like Milton's fallen angels, and Hyperion, the sun god, who has retained his powers, is their only hope for regaining their former glory. But, unfortunately for them, the Titans' era ends with the coming of Apollo, the Olympian god of poetry, music, and knowledge.

---

[49] Miltonic inversions, as displayed throughout Paradise Lost, involves inverting natural word order for effect. The most obvious example would be Milton's description of Hell as "darkness visible". The normal word order would be "visible darkness," but Milton inverts this order because he wants to emphasize the darkness of hell rather than its visibility. [Source: "*What is flunkeyism in W. M. Thackeray's works and Miltonic inversion in Paradise Lost?*", e-notes.]

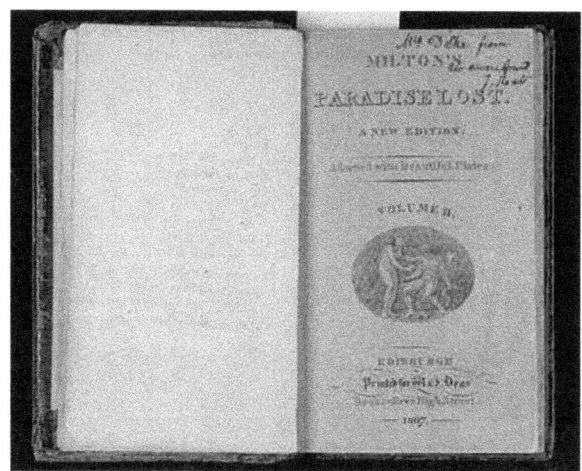

Keats's copy of Milton's 'Paradise Lost'
at Keats House Museum, Hampstead

The second version of Hyperion ("*The Fall of Hyperion: A Dream*") is one of the most remarkable pieces of writing in Keats's work. Keats composed '*Fall of Hyperion*' by reworking, expanding, and personally narrating lines from his earlier fragmented epic poem '*Hyperion*'. The poem begins with the narrator introducing the idea that the poem could be either a dream or a vision. The poem is divided into three scenes before its final fragmentation. It is narrated by the poet, who, in a dream, is allowed to enter a shrine. The goddess Moneta, the goddess of memory and the mother of the Muses, reveals to the dreamer that the function of the poet in the world is to separate himself from the mere dreamer and to enter into and embrace the suffering of humanity.[50]

The quality of Keats's blank verse in this poem reached new heights, particularly in the opening scene between *Thea* (Hyperion's sister)[51] and the fallen Saturn (King of Titans), rising to its height in the epiphany of the goddess Moneta, who reveals to the dreamer the function of the poet in the world.

Unfortunately, with the threat of approaching death upon him, Keats could not advance any further in the direction that he foresaw as the right one,

---

[50] "*Hyperion: work by Keats*", Encyclopedia Britannica.
[51] Thea is the Greek goddess of divine light. She is known for providing the gift of sight to mankind. It was believed that the beams of light from her eyes allowed others to see their destinies.

and the poem remains a 'fragment'. It was published in *Lamia, Isabella, The Eve of St. Agnes, and Other Poems* in 1820.

The plot and structure of The Fall of Hyperion has been greatly influenced by three previous epic works, Virgil's *'Aeneid'*, Milton's *'Paradise Lost'*, and Dante's *'Divine Comedy'*. The structure of the quest for knowledge is based on Dante's use of Virgil's descent into Hades[52], and the language and narration style reflects this. The language and detail style is also reminiscent of *'Paradise Lost'*, which, in many letters, Keats has stated was a quality epic, but dealt with morality on a simplistic level. The form and metre of Keats's epic is also similar to Milton's.[53]

Critique

Hyperion is rated as one of the greatest poems in the history of English literature, appreciated by poets, critics and writers; but ironically, it is called a fragment instead of an epic. A reading of the entire (incomplete) poem readily leads one to infer that the poem is a masterpiece. Its imagery, scenes, splendid characters, style, story, language and theme make it one of the best epic poems in English literature. Questions here arise that if everything was perfect then why did Keats leave it incomplete. Why didn't he complete it and surpass Milton in writing an epic poem at such a young age? What was the reason behind leaving the poem as a 'fragment'?

Keats was influenced by many writers, such as, Milton, Dante, Virgil and Spenser. Some other influences which can be found in *Hyperion* are Lemprier's classical dictionary[54], Hesiod's Theogony[55], Tooke's

---

[52] The underground abode of the dead.

[53] Bate, Walter Jackson. "*The Stylistic Development of Keats*", New York: Humanities Press, 1962.

[54] '*Lemprier's classical dictionary*' is a dictionary compiled by John Lempriere, containing a copious account of all the proper names mentioned in ancient authors, along with the value of coins, weights, and measures used among the Greeks and Romans, and a chronological table [See, Internet Archive. https://archive.org/details/aclassicaldicti00lempgoog]

[55] An account of the origin and descent of the gods.

pantheon[56], Ovid's metamorphoses[57], Chapman, Ronsard's A Michel de l' hospital, Davies's Leltic Reseraches, Beckford's Vathek[58], Annals of the Fine Arts[59].

As far as the design of poem is concerned, there is strong influence of Milton so much so that it seems that the poet instead of imitating life and mythology has imitated the *"Paradise Lost"*. The theme of Hyperon is also quite similar to one chosen by Milton in the *"Paradise Lost"*. Keats has written about the fall of Titans; while Milton has written about the fall of Satan; Keats, like Milton, has selected super human being for the purpose of writing an epic. Saturn, in Keats's Hyperion, is the leader of Titans, the fallen gods, whereas Satan is the ruler of fallen angels in Milton's *"Paradise Lost"*. In the beginning of *"Paradise Lost"*, we see fallen angels and in *Hyperion* we see fallen Titans. Hyperion is the only hope for the Titans in *Paradise Lost* as Satan is for the fallen angels in *"Paradise Lost"*. Subject matter of both the poems is dethronement and their effort to gain their position again. Apart from theme, characters and design, style of the poem is also Miltonic. It is not only influence rather undue influence of Milton on Keats, but also the language, metaphors, grand style and poetry of Milton that has been followed excessively.

---

[56] Tooke's Pantheon, full title '*Tooke's Pantheon of the Heathen Gods and Illustrious Heroes*', was a work on Greek mythology. Authored by the Jesuit François Pomey (1619–1673), the "*Pantheum mythicum seu fabulosa deorum historia*" became the mythological handbook of the following two centuries. [See, Wikipedia]

[57] The '*Metamorphoses*' is a Latin narrative poem from 8 CE by the Roman poet Ovid. It is considered his magnum opus. The poem chronicles the history of the world from its creation to the deification of Julius Caesar in a mythico-historical framework comprising over 250 myths, 15 books, and 11,995 lines. [See, Wikipedia]

[58]"*Vathek, an Arabian Tale*" or "*The History of the Caliph Vathek*" is a Gothic novel written by William Beckford, published in 1786. It Is considered a masterpiece of bizarre invention and sustained fantasy. It is a story of the caliph Vathek, a blasphemous voluptuary, who constructs a tower so tall that from it he can survey all the kingdoms of the world.

The novel chronicles the fall from power of the Caliph Vathek, who renounces Islam and engages with his mother, Carathis, in a series of licentious and deplorable activities designed to gain him supernatural powers. At the end of the novel, instead of attaining these powers, Vathek descends into a hell ruled by the fallen angel Eblis where he is doomed to wander endlessly and speechlessly.. [See, Encyclopedia Britannica, Wikipedia]

[59] A quarterly magazine issued in seventeen numbers, from about July 1816 to August 1820. This 'first attempt at a Journal of the Fine Arts' was edited by the architect and author, James Elmes (1782--1862). Through his friend Benjamin Haydon he came to know Keats, some of whose poetry was first published in this magazine.

John Milton

In *Hyperion*, Keats has blended the work of Milton and Spenser. He has seen Milton through the eyes of Spenser. He has definitely done justice to Spenser's work while adding language and description from his work. However, the imagery, stillness and picture drawing techniques in Spenser's work have greatly influenced Keats's work in *Hyperion*. Therefore, the poet, as such, failed to do poetic justice while writing *Hyperion* because of the excessive Spenserian and Miltonic influence on his work. In fact, the influence of other writers was so much that the poet himself realized that he was not doing poetic justice; therefore, he gave up the idea of writing an epic poem. In a letter Keats wrote: -

> *"I have given up Hyperion, there were too many Miltonic inversions in it—Miltonic verse cannot be written because it is an artist's humour and I wish to give myself up to other sensations. English ought to be kept up."*

Keats himself has given four reasons to leave the poem unfinished. First, he feels that he has not enough poetic maturity. Second, he is not doing poetic justice. Third, too much Spenser-Miltonic influence vitiates originality of the poem. Fourth, like Milton, he does not want to corrupt the English language.

These causes are enough for a poet to leave the idea of writing an epic poem. Furthermore, at the time he was writing *Hyperion*, Keats himself was of the view that he did not have enough poetic maturity to write an epic poem; he also felt that the influence of many other writers, especially Milton, was making his poem a copy instead of an original epic. Apart from these, Keats was of the opinion that Milton's language is artificial. He considered him the corruptor of English language; he didn't want to increase the corruption, therefore, left his work unfinished.[60][61]

In the end, with all its drawbacks, *Hyperion* is a masterpiece. It gives us a thesis of life in a concrete shape. Dealing with super-human beings, the poem retains its human character. It does not take us away from the world of man rather it helps us look at life with greater insight, and more than that poem has its own artistic beauty, which makes it a memorable literary piece.

In *Endymion* Keats had trailed the reader through an endless labyrinth of dreaming narrative and artistic description of amorous ardours. Its leisurely beauties seem to smother us under rose. In *Hyperion,* on the other hand, he decides to discard them, and adopts a style of bracing economy and elegance, Here, we have a narrative that stands out in classical pure and simple outline; and we have scenes and figures standing out as sculptural relief. *Hyperion* presents a Greek theme in the Greek manner, with Miltonic echoes—but at the same time, a new and original creation with merits and drawbacks all its own.

---

[60] *"Why John Keats's Hyperion is Called a Fragment?"*, published in 'Ask literature', November 9, 2018.

[61] Keats' impression of Milton as a "corruptor" of English language can be seen as a reflection of his concern that Milton's intricate and grandiose style might have had a negative impact on the natural simplicity and musicality of the English language. Keats, being a proponent of a more sensuous and vivid poetic style, might have perceived Milton's language as overly complex and removed from the immediate sensory experiences that Keats aimed to capture in his own poetry.

Keats' views are, however, not universally held, and many scholars and readers greatly admire Milton's contribution to English literature. Milton's epic poem "Paradise Lost" is considered one of the greatest achievements in English literature, and his influence on subsequent generations of poets and writers also has been profound.

Keats' critique of Milton is to be understood within the context of his own poetic goals and preferences, as well as the larger debates about poetic style and language that were occurring in the Romantic era. Literary criticism often involves differing perspectives, and these debates contribute to the richness and evolution of literature over time.

Keats was part of the Romantic movement, which valued emotions, individual experiences, and the beauty of nature. In this context, he might have seen Milton's elaborate and structured style as potentially stifling the natural flow of emotions and the imaginative quality he sought in poetry.

Chapter 9
Keats: More Masterpieces II

"A poet is the most unpoetical of anything in existence, because he has no Identity."

-- John Keats

"La Belle Dame Sans Merci" ("The Beautiful Lady Without Mercy") (1819)

"O what can ail thee, knight-at-arms,
Alone and palely loitering?
The sedge has withered from the lake,
And no birds sing.
O what can ail thee, knight-at-arms,
So haggard and so woe-begone?
The squirrel's granary is full,
And the harvest's done.
I see a lily on thy brow,
With anguish moist and fever-dew,
And on thy cheeks death's fading rose
Fast withereth too.
I met a lady in the meads,
Full beautiful—a faery's child,
Her hair was long, her foot was light,
And her eyes were wild.
I made a garland for her head,
And bracelets too, and fragrant zone;
She looked at me as she did love,

And made sweet moan.
I set her on my pacing steed,
And nothing else saw all day long,
For sidelong would she bend, and sing
A faery's song.
She found me roots of relish sweet,
And honey wild, and manna-dew,
And sure in language strange she said—
'I love thee true'.
She took me to her Elfin grot,
And there she wept and sighed full sore,
And there I shut her wild eyes
With kisses four
And there she lullèd me asleep,
And there I dreamed—Ah! woe betide! —
The latest dream I ever dreamt
On the cold hill side
I saw pale kings and princes too,
Pale warriors, death-pale were they all;
They cried— 'La Belle Dame sans Merci
Thee hath in thrall!'
I saw their starved lips in the gloam,
With horrid warning gapèd wide,
And I awoke and found me here,
On the cold hill's side.
And this is why I sojourn here,
Alone and palely loitering,
Though the sedge is withered from the lake,
And no birds sing."

[John Keats, *"La Belle Dame sans Merci"* (The Original version, 1819)]

It was the magical year 1819 once again. It was during this year in the beautiful ambience of English spring Keats wrote "*La Belle Dame Sans*

Merci" ("The Beautiful Lady Without Mercy"). It was about this time he had begun to realize the full literary potential of his genius and had embarked on an extraordinary creative spree. One by one several of his great masterpieces were written during this period, which would be published the following year. Tragically, it was during this period he exhibited the first symptoms of tuberculosis.

At the turn of the nineteenth century, "consumption", as pulmonary tuberculosis was commonly known, had evolved into a major public health concern throughout Europe, because of increasing urbanization. At its peak incidence, tuberculosis affected 70-90% of the urban population in Europe and accounted for nearly 40% of all deaths among the working class. Before the discovery of the intracellular *pathogen M. tuberculosis* by Robert Koch in 1882, 'consumption' was widely believed to be a hereditary illness rather than a contagious one, and precautions against its transmission were rarely taken.

Keats's family was one of the many households ravaged by tuberculosis. **Throughout his life, Keats** was possessed and pursued by death: He had witnessed death at several critical junctures of his life; beginning with his father's mysterious fall from a horse followed by the death of his **maternal uncle,** other and brother from the "family curse" - tuberculosis - that would eventually destroy him as well.

The poem *"La Belle Dame Sans Merci"* is a narrative of an enigmatic encounter that entails both pleasure and pain. Keats took this title from a medieval poem with the same name by the French poet Alain Chartier[62]. The poem is a saga of love and death in a bleak wintry landscape. It reveals the encounter between a knight, *'haggard and woe-begone'*, who stumbles upon a mysterious elfin beauty, a *"faery's child"*, during the winter month,

---

[62] Alain Chartier, (born c. 1385, Bayeux, Normandy, France—died c. 1433, Avignon, Provence?), French poet and political writer whose didactic, elegant, and Latinate style was regarded as a model by succeeding generations of poets and prose writers.

His work, written mainly from 1415 to 1430, is distinguished by its variety of subject matter and form. Chartier was a poet, orator, historian, moralist, and pamphleteer who wrote in Latin and French. Chartier's poems are mostly allegories in the courtly tradition but show the influence of his classical learning in their frequent Latinisms. They include *La Belle Dame sans merci*, *Le Lay de paix* ("The Lay of Peace"), and *Le Bréviaire des nobles*, the first of which, a tale of unrequited love, is the best known and was translated into English in the 15th century. [Source: Encyclopedia Britannica]

and after spending a night with her in an idyllic grotto, the knight woke up to find himself drained of his vitality. Thus at the end of his journey, the knight is on the brink of death all forlorn in a place where "*no birds sing*".

Alain Chartier

The mysterious femme fatale in the poem attracts lovers only to destroy them by her supernatural powers. She destroys for it is her nature to destroy. Keats perhaps found patterns for his "*faery's child*" in folk mythology, classical literature, or in the medieval ballad. With his masterly touches, he creates a woman who is beautiful, erotically attractive, fascinating, and deadly.

The poem reveals the obverse and destructive side of idyllic love and is sometimes seen as a counterpart to Keats's "*The Eve of St. Agnes*", which represents an idyllic view of love.

Some readers see the poem as Keats's personal rebellion against the pains of love. In his letters and in some of his poems, he reveals that he did experience pains, as well as pleasures, of love and that he resented the pains, particularly the loss of freedom that came with falling in love.

The poem *"La Belle Dame Sans Merci"* reflects Keats's painful familiarity with 'consumption'. In the opening three stanzas of the ballad, there is a graphic sketch of the knight's condition, which bears an uncanny resemblance to tubercular illness. His sickly pallor is highlighted by a cold pale forehead -- "*a lily on thy brow*", and colourless cheeks -- "*on thy cheeks a fading rose*"; and he is tormented by fatigue ("*haggard*"), fever, and night sweats -- "*anguish moist and fever- dew*", --- all signs of active tuberculosis.

La belle dame sans merci, 1893
-- painted by John William Waterhouse[63]

"*La Belle Dame Sans Merci*" is remarkable for both its rich sensual imagery and prophetic insight. Keats's desire for companionship, his fear of obscurity, and his awareness of imminent death are all allegorically encoded into the knight's struggle with solitude and mortality. Forsaken and terminally ill, Keats's knight has been reduced to living a "*posthumous existence*"—an experience Keats would share during the final months of his life. No birds sang his name when he died, and it would take another three decades for his genius to be recognized.

Keats wrote in a letter to his friend Richard Woodhouse, "*A poet is the most unpoetical of anything in existence, because he has no Identity.*" He was of the view that poets should be "*unpoetical*" and must strive to separate their personal identities from their narratives. But '*La Belle Dame Sans Merci*' shows that complete disengagement of an artist from his art is perhaps impossible. Keats himself, even though he had advocated for a stoic

---

[63] John William Waterhouse RA (6 April 1849 – 10 February 1917) was an English painter known for working first in the Academic style and for then embracing the Pre-Raphaelite Brotherhood's style and subject matter. [See, Wikipedia]

approach, failed to elude his own demons in the labyrinths of verse and allowed death to cast its shadow in his poem.

Keats was passionate for beauty and love. His passion for death was no less intense.

Chapter 10
Keats: More Masterpieces III

"Do not all charms fly
At the mere touch of philosophy?"

-- John Keats, 'Lamia'

Lamia (1819)

"*Lamia*" is another beautiful poem Keats wrote in 1819. It first appeared in the volume "*Lamia, Isabella, The Eve of St. Agnes, and Other Poems*" published in July 1820. It was composed soon after his '*La belle dame sans merci*' and his '*odes on Melancholy*', '*on Indolence*', '*on a Grecian Urn*' and '*to a Nightingale*' and just before '*To Autumn*'.

'*Lamia*' is a narrative poem written in rhymed couplets.[64] It was the last of Keats's three narrative poems. It is based on a story from the '*Anatomy of Melancholy*' by Robert Burton, which is based on a work by an ancient Greek writer. To some extent, Keats's personal frustration in love influences the poem. The poem, written in two parts, shares with Keats's other works the same thematic pattern, basic attitude to love, life and death, as well as a close connection with the poet's personal experience.

'*Lamia*' tells the story of how the god Hermes[65], on hearing of a nymph who is more beautiful than all, begins searching for her. In Part I, Hermes arrives in the forest of Crete to search for his beloved nymph. Here

---

[64] A couplet is a pair of lines in a verse that typically have the same meter or rhythm and usually complete one thought.

[65] Hermes is an Olympian deity in ancient Greek religion In myth, Hermes functions as the emissary and messenger of the gods, and is considered the son of Zeus and Maia. He is also believed to be the protector of human heralds, travellers, thieves, merchants, and orators. He is able to move quickly and freely between the worlds of the mortal and the divine aided by his winged sandals. Hermes also plays the role of the psychopomp or "soul guide"—a conductor of souls into the afterlife. [See, Wikipedia]

he meets Lamia the serpent-woman who promises to reveal the presence of his nymph to him if he gave her a woman's body and placed her near Corinth. Hermes agrees. The nymph is revealed to Hermes, who, in his turn, changes Lamia, the serpent-woman, into a beautiful maiden and places her on the road to Corinth.

On the way to Corinth, Lamia sees Lycius, a young, handsome Corinthian youth, and she falls in love with him, while Hermes and his nymph depart together into the woods. The young Lycius too falls in love with Lamia. He tells her that he would die if the vision of their love were to vanish. Together they go to Corinth and begin to live happily in the blisses of love in a palatial building, created by the magical power of Lamia.

In Part II, Lycius decides they ought to marry and invite all their friends to their bridal feast. Lamia is strongly opposed to this plan, but at the insistence of Lycius, she relents on the condition that Lycius will not invite his friend philosopher Apollonius to the marriage feast.

While Lycius is absent to invite all his kinsfolk to the wedding, Lamia, with her magic powers, summons invisible servants who decorate the banquet room and furnish it with rich foods of every kind. When Lycius's guests arrive, they marvel at the splendour of the mansion. None of them had known that there was such a magnificent palace in Corinth. And among the guests is Apollonius, who has arrived uninvited.

'The Kiss of the Enchantress' (Isobel Lilian Gloag, c. 1890), inspired by Keats's Lamia, depicts Lamia as half-serpent, half-woman[66]

At the height of the wedding feast, Apollonius begins to stare fixedly at Lamia. Lamia grows pale and exhibits extreme discomfort. She makes no answer to Lycius's anxious questions as to what ails her. The feasting and the music come to a stop. Turning to Apollonius, Lycius commands him to cease staring at Lamia. "*Fool*," answers the philosopher contemptuously,

"from every ill
Of life have I preserv'd thee to this day,
And shall I see thee made a serpent's prey?"

Looking at Lamia again, he utters two words: "*A serpent!*" At the words, Lamia utters a dreadful scream, dissolves into a snake and then vanishes, while a heartbroken Lycius being grief-stricken dies.

"*Lamia*" shows narrative power, and Keats's ability to write a closely-knit story in verse. The theme of the poem has obvious similarities to that of Coleridge's "*Christabel*"[67]. But Keats's treatment has a sense of stark reality amidst enchantment. Keats once wrote in a letter, "*Oh, for a life of sensations rather than of thought!*" He believed imagination, passion, and experience

---

[66] Isobel Lilian Gloag was an English Victorian painter, known for her oil and watercolour portraits, as well as posters and stained-glass designs.

[67] In "*Christabel*", a long narrative ballad by Samuel Taylor Coleridge written between 1797 (Part I) and 1800 (Part II), the central female character 'Christabel' goes into the woods to pray by a large oak tree, where she hears a strange noise. Upon looking behind the tree, she finds Geraldine who says that she had been abducted from her home by men on horseback. Christabel pities her and takes her home with her. However, supernatural signs, like, a dog angrily moaning despite being asleep, fading flames on torches suddenly reigniting, Geraldine being unable to cross an iron gate, denial of prayer, etc.- seem to indicate that all is not well. They spend the night together, but while Geraldine undresses, she shows a terrible but undefined mark:
"*Behold! her bosom and half her side—*
A sight to dream of, not to tell! /
And she is to sleep by Christabel" (Line, 246–48).
Christabel's father, Sir Leoline, however, becomes enthralled with Geraldine and orders a grand procession to announce her rescue. He ignores the weak objections of his daughter, who, although under enchantment, is starting to realize the enormity of Geraldine's malign nature. The unfinished poem ends here. [See, Wikipedia]

could reveal truth better than cold reasoning. This is in keeping with the theme of "*Lamia*," which makes thought and reason the antitheses of passion and imagination.

Samuel Taylor Coleridge

Influence

The poem '*Lamia*' inspired symphonic poems by Edward MacDowell (1888)[68] and Dorothy Howell (1918).

Keats's '*Lamia*' also had a deep influence on Edgar Allan Poe's sonnet "*To Science*", specifically the following passage that discusses the baleful effects of "*cold philosophy*". The "*cold philosopher*" Apollonius kills both Lycius and Lamia.

"Lamia"

"... Do not all charms fly
At the mere touch of cold philosophy?
There was an awful rainbow once in heaven:
We know her woof, her texture; she is given

---

[68] Edward MacDowell. Lamia, Op.29, score at IMSLP.

In the dull catalogue of common things.
Philosophy will clip an Angel's wings,
Conquer all mysteries by rule and line,
Empty the haunted air, and gnomed mine—
Unweave a rainbow, as it erewhile made
The tender-person'd Lamia melt into a shade."

[John Keats, *'Lamia'* lines 229–238]

Poe's closing lines in the sonnet *"To Science"* also echo several lines near the middle of "*Lamia*".[69][70]

"Sonnet -- To Science" (1829) By Edgar Allan Poe

"*Science! true daughter of Old Time thou art!*
Who alterest all things with thy peering eyes.
Why preyest thou thus upon the poet's heart,
Vulture, whose wings are dull realities?
How should he love thee? or how deem thee wise,
Who wouldst not leave him in his wandering
To seek for treasure in the jewelled skies,
Albeit he soared with an undaunted wing?
Hast thou not dragged Diana from her car,
And driven the Hamadryad from the wood
To seek a shelter in some happier star?
Hast thou not torn the Naiad from her flood,
The Elfin from the green grass, and from me
The summer dream beneath the tamarind tree?"

Beauty through the lens of science: "…Do I see less or more?"

---

[69] Campbell, Killis. "*The Origins of Poe*", The Mind of Poe and Other Studies. New York: Russell & Russell, Inc., 1962, pp. 154–155.

[70] "*Sonnet — To Science*" is an 1829 poem by Edgar Allan Poe, published in Al Aaraaf, Tamerlane, and Minor Poems.

> *"Newton, Keats agreed with Lamb, had destroyed all the poetry of the rainbow, by reducing it to the prismatic colours. ... Newton's dissection of the rainbow into light of different wavelengths led on to Maxwell's theory of electromagnetism and thence to Einstein's theory of special relativity. If you think the rainbow has poetic mystery, you should try relativity."*
>
> -- Richard Dawkins, *"Unweaving the Rainbow"*

The book *"Unweaving the Rainbow: Science, Delusion and the Appetite for Wonder"* (1998) by Richard Dawkins also, under the influence of Keats, takes its title from *Lamia*. It, however, seeks to demonstrate that science reveals, rather than destroys, the true beauty of the natural world.[71] Interestingly, it reminds us of the Nobel-winning physicist Richard Feynman who, in a similar context, had brilliantly asked:

> *"Poets say science takes away from the beauty of the stars — mere globs of gas atoms. I too can see the stars on a desert night, and feel them. But do I see less or more?"*[72]

And then expounding further his own views on the subject, he asserted:

> *"The vastness of the heavens stretches my imagination — stuck on this carousel my little eye can catch one-million-year-old light. A vast pattern — of which I am a part [...] What is the pattern, or the meaning, or the why? It does not do harm to the mystery to know a little about it. For far more marvellous is the truth than any artists of the past imagined it. Why do the poets of the present not speak of it? What men are poets who can speak of Jupiter if he were a man, but if he is an immense spinning sphere of methane and ammonia must be silent?"*

Feynman refutes the notion that a scientific inquiry into physical reality bereaves life of the poetic; to the contrary — any poetry that fails to convey the inherent beauty and enchantment of scientific understanding, he suggests,

---

[71] Dawkins, Richard: *"Unweaving the Rainbow"*, Boston, Mass.: Houghton Mifflin. Passim, 1998.

[72] Feynman, Richard: *"The Relation of Physics to Other Sciences"* Six Easy Pieces: Essentials of Physics Explained by Its Most Brilliant Teacher, 1995.

is the result of an impoverished poetic imagination.[73] Science greatly enhances the ability to appreciate the beauty, he strongly believed. About two decades later, Feynman would build on these ideas in his now-iconic reflection known as "*Ode to a Flower*".[74][75]

Richard P. Feynman

---

[73] Popova, Maria: "*The World's Most Lyrical Footnote: Physicist Richard Feynman on the Life-Expanding Common Ground Between the Scientific and the Poetic Worldviews*", Marginalian.

[74] Popova, Maria: "*Ode to a Flower: Richard Feynman's Famous Monologue on Knowledge and Mystery, Animated*", The Marginalian.

[75] "Ode To A Flower" is an animation created by Fraser Davidson of Cub Studio. The quote, by Nobel Prize-winning physicist Richard Feynman, was given in 1981 during the CalTech professor's BBC interview for "*Horizon: The Pleasure of Finding Things Out*". [See, "Richard Feynman's 'Ode To A Flower' quote, animated", TKSST (The Kid Should See This), https://shorturl.at/iTV28]

> ## *"Ode to a Flower" (1981)*
>
> ## *Richard Feynman"*
>
> *"I have a friend who's an artist and has sometimes taken a view which I don't agree with very well. He'll hold up a flower and say "look how beautiful it is," and I'll agree. Then he says "I as an artist can see how beautiful this is but you as a scientist take this all apart and it becomes a dull thing," and I think that he's kind of nutty. First of all, the beauty that he sees is available to other people and to me too, I believe...*
> *I can appreciate the beauty of a flower. At the same time, I see much more about the flower than he sees. I could imagine the cells in there, the complicated actions inside, which also have a beauty. I mean it's not just beauty at this dimension, at one centimeter; there's also beauty at smaller dimensions, the inner structure, also the processes. The fact that the colors in the flower evolved in order to attract insects to pollinate it is interesting; it means that insects can see the color. It adds a question: does this aesthetic sense also exist in the lower forms? Why is it aesthetic? All kinds of interesting questions which the science knowledge only adds to the excitement, the mystery and the awe of a flower. It only adds. I don't understand how it subtracts."*

So does science really enable one to see more, and not less? Or, is it a 'cold philosophy' where the "*cold philosopher*" Apollonius kills both Lycius and Lamia?

In his "*Ode on a Grecian Urn*", Keats wrote: "*Beauty is truth, truth is beauty*'. But, where does the truth, in this case, really lie?" No one knows for sure. Perhaps it would be the best to leave it to the reader for, as the Irish novelist Margaret Wolfe Hungerford famously said, "*Beauty* (and hence, truth) *lies in the eyes of the beholder.*"

Chapter 11
Keats: 1819 Odes

"Heard melodies are sweet, but those unheard, are sweeter"

-- John Keats

In 1819, John Keats composed six odes, which are among his most famous and well-regarded poems. He wrote the first five poems, "*Ode on a Grecian Urn*", "*Ode on Indolence*", "*Ode on Melancholy*", "*Ode to a Nightingale*", and "*Ode to Psyche*" in quick succession during the spring, and composed the sixth one -- "*To Autumn*" ---- in September. The poems were transcribed by Brown, who later provided copies to the publisher Richard Woodhouse. Their exact date of composition is unknown; Keats simply dated "*Ode on a Grecian Urn*" May 1819, and did the same to its companion odes. The five poems as such display a unity in stanza forms and themes, but the unity fails to provide clear evidence of the order in which they were composed.

The odes, as a whole, represent Keats's attempt to create a new type of short lyrical poem, which influenced later generations. Through these odes, the poet describes the romance of Psyche, melodious songs of the Nightingale, the beauty and charm of Grecian art and the changing human moods.

Keats's odes move between two worlds; the real and the ideal world. Ideal world is one that every person has in mind and wishes to live in. The real world is an entirely different story, based on events that occur on the ground. The real-world deviates from the ideal depending on the local circumstances. The ideal world is our dream and the real world is actual.

After writing "*Ode to Psyche*", Keats sent the poem to his brother and explained his new ode form:

> "*I have been endeavouring to discover a better Sonnet stanza than we have. The legitimate does not suit the language well, from the*

pouncing rhymes; the other appears too elegiac, and the couplet at the end of it has seldom a pleasing effect. I do not pretend to have succeeded. It will explain itself."[76]

Why should we explore Keats's Odes separately from his other works?

While all of Keats's poetry has his signature spunk, many scholars argue that due to similarities in theme and psychological development, his odes seem to form a group together. The odes do not exactly tell a story; there is no unifying "plot" and no recurring characters, and there is little evidence that Keats intended them to stand together as a single work of art. Nevertheless, the extraordinary number of suggestive interrelations between them is impossible to ignore.[77] To the discerning reader, it would seem that the odes explore and develop the same themes, partake of many similar approaches and images, and, ordered in a certain way, to exhibit an unmistakable psychological development. This is not to say that the poems do not stand on their own—they do, magnificently; one of the greatest felicities of the sequence is that it can be entered at any point, viewed wholly or partially from any perspective, and still prove moving and rewarding to read. There has also been a great deal of critical debate over how to treat the voices that speak the poems. Are they meant to be read as though a single person speaks them all, or did Keats invent a different persona for each ode?[78]

Early in 1819, Keats left his position as dresser (or assistant house surgeon) at Guy's Hospital, Southwark, London and completely devoted himself to a career in poetry. In the past, he had relied on his brother George for financial assistance from time to time, but now his brother himself was in the grip of financial crisis. He needed money and appealed to Keats for financial help. But having left the career in medicine, Keats too, because of his own financial woes, was now unable to help his brother and was, therefore, overwhelmed with guilt and despair. At one point, he even decided

---

[76] Keats, John, *"The Life and Letters of John Keats"*, ed. Richard Houghton (reprint). Read Books, 2008, p.162.

[77] *"Keats's Odes"*, British Literature Wiki.

[78] *"John Keats and Keats's Odes Background"*, in 'Keats's Odes', Sparknotes,

to forsake the life of a poet for a more lucrative career – but not before allowing himself a few months of poetic indulgence.

Surprisingly, in spite of the difficult time he was going through, it was during the months of spring 1819 Keats wrote most of his major odes. Following the month of May 1819, he began to tackle other forms of poetry, including a play, some longer pieces, and a return to his unfinished epic, *Hyperion*. Though because of the crisis he was faced with, he had little energy or inclination left in him for composition, but, even then, on 19 September 1819, he managed to compose "*To Autumn*", his last major work and the one that rang the curtain down on his career as a poet.

Ode on a Grecian Urn

> **"Beauty is truth, truth beauty,—that is all**
> **Ye know on earth, and all ye need to know."**
>
> **- John Keats, "Ode On A Grecian Urn"**

The "*Ode on a Grecian Urn*" was written by Keats in May 1819, first published anonymously in *Annals of the Fine Arts* for 1819.

"Ode on a Grecian Urn"

> *"Thou still unravish'd bride of quietness,*
> *Thou foster-child of silence and slow time,*
> *Sylvan historian, who canst thus express*
> *A flowery tale more sweetly than our rhyme:*
> *What leaf-fring'd legend haunts about thy shape*
> *Of deities or mortals, or of both,*
> *In Tempe or the dales of Arcady?*
> *What men or gods are these? What maidens loth?*
> *What mad pursuit? What struggle to escape?*
> *What pipes and timbrels? What wild ecstasy?"*
>
> [John Keats, "*Ode on a Grecian Urn*", lines 1—10]

Keats was inspired to write the poem "*Ode on a Grecian Urn*" after reading two articles by English artist and writer Benjamin Haydon published in '*The*

Examiner' on 2 May and 9 May, 1819 respectively. In the first article, Haydon described Greek sacrifice and worship, and in the second article, he contrasted the artistic styles of *Raphael* and *Michelangelo* in conjunction with a discussion of medieval sculptures. Keats also had access to prints of Greek urns at Haydon's office, and he traced an engraving of the "*Sosibios Vase*" in The Louvre,[79] which he found in Henry Moses's *A Collection of Antique Vases*, Altars, Paterae, Tripods, Candelabra Sarcophagi, etc.[80] Thus, through his reading of various articles and art literature in this field as well as his own first-hand acquaintance with the *Elgin Marbles*[81], Keats perceived the idealism and representation of Greek virtues in classical Greek art, and his poem draws upon these insights.

In his *Ode on a Grecian Urn*, composed of in five stanzas of ten lines each, Keats addresses an ancient Greek urn, describing and discoursing upon the images depicted on it. In particular he reflects upon two scenes, one in which a lover pursues his beloved, and another where villagers and a priest gather to perform a sacrifice. The poet concludes with the observation that with the passage of time, there will be new generations, but the urn shall remain as a friend in the midst of other woes and will have the following to say to the future generations of mankind:

> "*When old age shall this generation waste,*
> *Thou shalt remain, in midst of other woe*
> *Than ours, a friend to man, to whom thou say'st,*
> *"Beauty is truth, truth beauty,—that is all*
> *Ye know on earth, and all ye need to know."*

---

[79] The 'Sosibios Vase' is a Neo-Attic marble krater of the Hellenistic period. It is attributed by signature to Sosibios, a Greek sculptor who was active in Rome during the end of the Roman Republic, and is dated to approximately 50 BCE.[See, Wikipedia]

[80] Moses, Henry: "*A Collection of Antique Vases, Altars, Paterae, Tripods, Candelabra Sarcophagi, etc.*", J. Taylor London, c.1823.

[81] The "*Elgin Marbles*" are a collection of Ancient Greek sculptures from the Parthenon and other structures from the Acropolis of Athens, removed from Ottoman Greece to Britain by agents of Thomas Bruce, 7th Earl of Elgin, and now held in the British Museum. The majority of the sculptures were created in the 5th century BCE under the direction of sculptor and architect Phidias. [Source: Wikipedia]

"Sosibios Vase", Krater, Louvre, Paris

"*Ode on a Grecian Urn*" was not well received by contemporary critics. It was only by the mid-19th century that it began to be praised, and it is now considered to be one of the greatest odes in the English language.

Although "*Ode on a Grecian Urn*" was completed in May 1819, its first printing came in January 1820 when it was published with "*Ode to a Nightingale*" in the *Annals of Fine Art*, an art magazine that promoted views on art similar to those Keats held. Following the initial publication, '*The Examiner*" published Keats's ode together with Haydon's two previously published articles. Keats also included the poem in his 1820 collection *Lamia, Isabella, The Eve of St Agnes, and Other Poems*.

Ode to Psyche

"I am certain of nothing but the holiness of the heart's affections, and the truth of imagination."

-- John Keats

"*Ode to Psyche*" by Keats is a tribute to the Greek goddess *Psyche*, the goddess of the soul, with whom Cupid fell in love.[82]

The speaker opens the poem with an address to the goddess *Psyche*, urging her to hear his words, and that she forgive him for singing to her own secrets. He says that while wandering through the forest that very day, he stumbled upon "*two fair creatures*" lying side by side in the grass, beneath a "*whisp'ring roof*" of leaves, surrounded by flowers. They embraced each another with both their arms and wings, and though their lips did not touch, they were close to one another and ready "*past kisses to outnumber.*" The speaker says he knew the winged boy, the Cupid, but asks who the girl was. And then he proceeds to answer his own question: She was *Psyche*.

Cupid and Psyche

---

[82] The poem does not describe the plot of the original Cupid and Psyche myth. According to Harold Bloom, the poem "has little to do with the accepted myth" [See: Bloom, Harold. "*The Visionary Company*", Ithaca: Cornell University Press, 1993, p.399].
In the original myth, Aphrodite punishes Psyche, a well admired girl, by having Cupid use his power to make her fall in love. Cupid, instead, falls in love with her, but he could only be with her in the cover of darkness in order to disguise his identity. Curious, she uses a light to reveal Cupid's identity, but he flees from her presence. Psyche begins to search after Cupid, and Aphrodite forces her to perform various tasks before she could be united with her love. After nearly dying from one of the tasks, Cupid asks Zeus, the King of Gods, to transform Psyche into a goddess so the two can be together.

In the second stanza, the speaker addresses Psyche again, describing her as the youngest and most beautiful of all the Olympian gods and goddesses. He believes this, he says, despite the fact that, unlike other divinities, Psyche has none of the trappings of worship: She has no temples, no altars, no choir to sing for her, and so on. And all these are due to Psyche's youth; she has come into the world too late for "*antique vows*" and the "*fond believing lyre.*" But the speaker says that even in the fallen days of his own time, he would like to pay homage to Psyche and become her choir, her music, and her oracle. And that he will become Psyche's priest and build her a temple in an "*untrodden region*" of his mind, a region surrounded by thought that resemble the beauty of nature and tended by "*the gardener Fancy*," or imagination. He promises Psyche "*all soft delight*" and says that the window of her new abode will be left open at night, so that her winged boy—"*the warm Love*"—can come in.

"Ode to Psyche"

"Yes, I will be thy priest, and build a fane
In some untrodden region of my mind,
Where branched thoughts, new grown with pleasant pain,
Instead of pines shall murmur in the wind:
Far, far around shall those dark-cluster'd trees
Fledge the wild-ridged mountains steep by steep;
And there by zephyrs, streams, and birds, and bees,
The moss-lain Dryads shall be lull'd to sleep;
And in the midst of this wide quietness
A rosy sanctuary will I dress
With the wreath'd trellis of a working brain,
With buds, and bells, and stars without a name,
With all the gardener Fancy e'er could feign,
Who breeding flowers, will never breed the same:
And there shall be for thee all soft delight
That shadowy thought can win,
A bright torch, and a casement ope at night,
To let the warm Love in!"

[John Keats, "*Ode to Psyche*"]

Ode to a Nightingale

"O for a life of Sensations rather than of Thoughts!"

-- **John Keats**

> **"Ode to a Nightingale"**
>
> *"My heart aches, and a drowsy numbness pains*
> *My sense, as though of hemlock I had drunk,*
> *Or emptied some dull opiate to the drains*
> *One minute past, and Lethe-wards had sunk:*
> *'Tis not through envy of thy happy lot,*
> *But being too happy in thine happiness,—*
> *That thou, light-winged Dryad of the trees*
> *In some melodious plot*
> *Of beechen green, and shadows numberless,*
> *Singest of summer in full-throated ease."*
>
> [John Keats, *"Ode to a Nightingale"*, lines 1–10]

"Ode to a Nightingale" reveals the highest imaginative powers of John Keats. The song of the nightingale moves from the poet to the depth of his heart and creates numbness. When he hears the song, he is embraced by the sweetness of his joy and the feeling becomes so excessive that it changes into a kind of pleasant pain and he is filled with a desire to escape from world of caring to the world of beautiful. Keats immortalizes the bird by imagining it as the symbol of universal and undying musical voice. This universal and eternal voice that has comforted human beings embittered by life and tragedies by opening the casement of the remote, magical, spiritual, eternal and ideal.[83]

Keats in this poem is trying to escape from the reality and experience the ideal. He makes imaginative flight into the ideal world but accepts the realities of life despite its fury. He soars high with his wings of poesy into the world of ideals and perfect happiness. But the next moment consciousness

---

[83] Mythili S & Suganya, John M.: *"The Real and Ideal World in The Odes of John Keats"*, Journal of Emerging Technologies and Innovative Research (JETIR), Volume 8, Issue 12, December 2021

makes him land on the grounds of reality and he bids farewell to the ideal bird. In fact, no one can escape into the ideal world forever. Imaginative minds can only have a momentary flight into the fanciful world. But ultimately one has to return to the real world and must accept the reality.

According to his friend Brown, "*Ode to a Nightingale*" was composed by the poet under a plum tree in the garden. Brown wrote,

> "*In the spring of 1819 a nightingale had built her nest near my house. Keats felt a tranquil and continual joy in her song; and one morning he took his chair from the breakfast-table to the grass-plot under a plum-tree, where he sat for two or three hours. When he came into the house, I perceived he had some scraps of paper in his hand, and these he was quietly thrusting behind the books. On inquiry, I found those scraps, four or five in number, contained his poetic feelings on the song of our nightingale.*"[84]

Joseph Severn's painting of Keats
'Listening to the Nightingale on Hampstead Heath', c. 1845,

---

[84] Bate, Walter Jackson: "*John Keats*". Cambridge, Mass.: Harvard University Press, 1964.

Dilke, co-owner of the house (with Brown), however, strenuously denied Brown's story, printed in Richard Monckton Milnes' 1848 biography of Keats, dismissing it as *"pure delusion"*.[85]

The "*Ode to a Nightingale*" is a description of Keats's journey into the state of 'negative capability', a concept evolved by the poet himself.[86] The tone of the poem rejects the optimistic pursuit of pleasure found within Keats's earlier poems and, instead, explores the themes of nature, transience and mortality, the latter being particularly relevant to Keats. The nightingale described experiences a type of death but does not actually die. Instead, the songbird is capable of living through its song. The poem ends with an acceptance that pleasure cannot last and that death is an inevitable part of life.

Ode on Melancholy

"She dwells with Beauty—Beauty that must die;

And Joy, whose hand is ever at his lips

Bidding adieu; and aching Pleasure nigh,

Turning to poison while the bee-mouth sips [...]"

-- John Keats, "Ode on Melancholy"

The "*Ode on Melancholy*" addresses the subject of how to cope with sadness. The first stanza tells what not to do: The sufferer should not "*go to Lethe,*"[87] or forget their sadness; should not commit *suicide*[88]; and should not become obsessed with *objects of death and misery*[89] (*the beetle, the death-moth, and the owl*). For, the speaker says, that will make the anguish of the soul drowsy, while the sufferer should do everything he can to remain aware of and alert to the depths of his suffering.

---

[85] Gittings, Robert: *"The odes of Keats and their earliest known manuscripts in Facsimile"*, Kent State University Press, 1970.

[86] See, Chapter 14: *"Letters of John Keats (1816-21)"*.

[87] '*Lethe'* in Greek mythology is a river in Hades whose waters cause drinkers to forget their past. Lethe thus means oblivion, forgetfulness [See, Merriam – Webster Dictionary].

[88] '*nightshade*', "*the ruby grape of Prosperpine,*" is a poison; Prosperpine is the mythological queen of the underworld.

[89] Objects of death and misery: *the beetle, the death-moth, and the owl.*

"*Ode on Melancholy*"

"No, no, go not to Lethe, neither twist
Wolf's-bane, tight-rooted, for its poisonous wine;
Nor suffer thy pale forehead to be kiss'd
By nightshade, ruby grape of Proserpine;
Make not your rosary of yew-berries,
Nor let the beetle, nor the death-moth be
Your mournful Psyche, nor the downy owl
A partner in your sorrow's mysteries;
For shade to shade will come too drowsily,
And drown the wakeful anguish of the soul.

But when the melancholy fit shall fall
Sudden from heaven like a weeping cloud,
That fosters the droop-headed flowers all,
And hides the green hill in an April shroud;
Then glut thy sorrow on a morning rose,
Or on the rainbow of the salt sand-wave,
Or on the wealth of globed peonies;
Or if thy mistress some rich anger shows,
Emprison her soft hand, and let her rave,
And feed deep, deep upon her peerless eyes."

[John Keats, "*Ode on Melancholy*", lines 1-20]

"*Ode on melancholy*" is one of Keats's greatest insights into the nature of human experience. In this poem, the two conflicting domains of consciousness manifest as joy and melancholy. The underlying idea of the poem is that sadness is to be found not in the ugly and painful things of life but in the beauty and pleasures of the world. The remedy for melancholy is, therefore, something that makes one unconscious of sadness and pain. To experience melancholy, one must stimulate all senses and only greater consciousness can make us experience true melancholy and tragedies of life. The originality in Keats's conception in this ode lies in the simultaneity of perception. Keats believes that the natural world is the only one mortals can access and that there is no escape from melancholy.

'She dwells with Beauty—Beauty that must die'
Illustration to the poem "Ode on Melancholy" by John Keats – From 'Poems of Keats', Published c. 1910.

Ode on Indolence

"[…] *I burn'd And ached for wings* […]"

-- John Keats, "Ode on Indolence"

By the spring of 1819, Keats had left his position as an Assistant surgeon at Guy's Hospital, Southwark, London, to devote himself to poetry. On 12 May 1819, however, he abandoned this plan after receiving a request for financial assistance from his brother, George. Unable to help, Keats was severely torn by guilt and despair. It was under these circumstances that he wrote "*Ode on Indolence*". In a letter to his brother dated 19 March 1819, Keats had discussed '*indolence*' as a subject. He may, therefore, have written the ode as early as March, but the themes and stanza forms suggest May or June 1819; when he was working on his other odes, such as, "*Ode on a Grecian Urn*", "*Ode on Melancholy*", "*Ode to a Nightingale*" and "*Ode to Psyche*". During this period, Keats's friend Charles Armitage Brown transcribed copies of the spring odes and submitted them to publisher Richard

Woodhouse. Keats also wrote to his friend Sarah Jeffrey: "[T]*he thing I have most enjoyed this year has been writing an ode to Indolence.*"[90]

The "*Ode on Indolence*" is one of five odes composed by Keats in the spring of 1819. But unlike the other odes he wrote that year, "*Ode on Indolence*" was not published until 1848, 27 years after his death.

Keats's notes and papers do not reveal the precise dating of the 1819 odes. Literary scholars have proposed several different orders of composition, arguing that the poems form a sequence within their structures. In *The Consecrated Urn*, Bernard Blackstone observes that "*Indolence*" has been variously thought the first, second, and final of the five 1819 odes.[91] Biographer Robert Gittings suggests "*Ode on Indolence*" was written on 4 May 1819, based upon Keats's report about the weather during the ode's creation;[92] Douglas Bush insists it was written after "*Nightingale*", "*Grecian Urn*", and "*Melancholy*".[93] Based on his examination of the stanza forms, Keats biographer Andrew Motion thinks "*Ode on Indolence*" was written after "*Ode to Psyche*" and "*Ode to a Nightingale*", although he admits there is no way to be precise about the dates. Nevertheless, he argues that "*Ode on Indolence*" was probably composed last.[94]

The "*Ode on Indolence*" is an example of Keats's break from the structure of the classical form. It portrays the poet's contemplation of a morning spent in idleness. Three figures are presented—*Ambition, Love* and *Poesy*—dressed in "*placid sandals*" and "*white robes*". The narrator examines each one using a series of questions and statements on life and art:

"*Ode on Indolence*"

> "*One morn before me were three figures seen,*
> *With bowed necks, and joined hands, side-faced;*
> *And one behind the other stepp'd serene,*
> *In placid sandals, and in white robes graced;*

---

[90] 'Letter to Sarah Jeffrey'. 9 June 1819. Colvin 1970 qtd. p. 356.
[91] Blackstone, Bernard. "*The Consecrated Urn*", Longmans Green: London (1959).
[92] Gittings, Robert. "*John Keats*", London: Heinemann, 1968, pp.311-313.
[93] Bush, Douglas. "*John Keats: His Life and Writings*", London: Macmillan, 1966, p.148.
[94] Motion, Andrew: "*Keats*", London: Faber, 1997

> *They pass'd, like figures on a marble urn,*
> *When shifted round to see the other side;*
> *They came again; as when the urn once more*
> *Is shifted round, the first seen shades return;*
> *And they were strange to me, as may betide*
> *With vases, to one deep in Phidian lore.*
> *How is it, Shadows! that I knew ye not?*
> *How came ye muffled in so hush a mask?*
> *Was it a silent deep-disguisèd plot*
> *To steal away, and leave without a task*
> *My idle days? Ripe was the drowsy hour;*
> *The blissful cloud of summer-indolence*
> *Benumb'd my eyes; my pulse grew less and less;*
> *Pain had no sting, and pleasure's wreath no flower:*
> *O, why did ye not melt, and leave my sense*
> *Unhaunted quite of all but—nothingness?*
> *A third time pass'd they by, and, passing, turn'd*
> *Each one the face a moment whiles to me;*
> *Then faded, and to follow them I burn'd*
> *And ached for wings, because I knew the three;*
> *The first was a fair Maid, and Love her name;*
> *The second was Ambition, pale of cheek,*
> *And ever watchful with fatiguèd eye;*
> *The last, whom I love more, the more of blame*
> *Is heap'd upon her, maiden most unmeek,—*
> *I knew to be my demon Poesy."*
>
> [John Keats, "*Ode on Indolence*", lines 1--30]

As the poem progresses, the narrator begins to discuss the intrusion upon his indolence by the figures of Love, Ambition, and Poesy, and he suggests that the images have come to "steal away" his idle days.

The poet wishes to be with the three figures, but he is unable to join them. The poem transitions into the narrator providing reasons why he would not need the three figures, and while he is able to do so with ambition and love, he cannot find a reason to dismiss poesy.

Tracing of an engraving of the Sosibios vase by John Keats.

The figures of "*Ode on Indolence*" are described as similar to those from an urn.

In the final stanzas, the figure of Poesy is described as a 'daemon' which Helen Vendler suggests poses a direct threat to the idleness the poet wishes to retain.[95] Finally, the narrator declares that the figures should be treated as figures, and they should better vanish from his idle spright into the clouds, and never again return for he would not be misled by them:

> *"So, ye three Ghosts, adieu! Ye cannot raise*
> *My head cool-bedded in the flowery grass;*
> *For I would not be dieted with praise,*
> *A pet-lamb in a sentimental farce!*
> *Fade softly from my eyes, and be once more*

---

[95] Vendler, Helen. "*The Odes of John Keats*". Cambridge, Massachusetts: Harvard University Press, 1983, p. 20.

In masque-like figures on the dreary urn;
Farewell! I yet have visions for the night,
And for the day faint visions there is store;
Vanish, ye Phantoms! from my idle spright,
Into the clouds, and never more return!"

[John Keats, *"Ode on Indolence"*, lines 51–60]

Literary critics regard "*Ode on Indolence*" as inferior to Keats's other 1819 odes. Walter Evert wrote that "*it is unlikely that the 'Ode on Indolence' has ever been anyone's favourite poem, and it is certain that it was not Keats's. Why he excluded it from the 1820 volume we do not know, but it is repetitious and declamatory and structurally infirm, and these would be reasons enough.*"[96] According to Bate, the poem's value is "*primarily biographical and not poetic*".[97]

In 1973, Stuart Sperry described the poem as "*a rich and nourishing immersion in the rush of pure sensation and its flow of stirring shadows and 'dim dreams'. In many ways the ode marks both a beginning and an end. It is both the feeblest and potentially the most ambitious of the sequence. Yet its failure, if we choose to consider it that, is more the result of deliberate disinclination than any inability of means.*"[98] Andrew Motion, in 1997, argued, "*Like 'Melancholy', the "Ode on Indolence" is also too articulate for its own poetic good ... In two of his May odes, 'Melancholy' and 'Indolence', Keats defined themes common to the whole group with such fierce candour that he restricted their imaginative power. His identity had prevailed.*"[99]

To Autumn

"The poetry of the earth is never dead."

- John Keats

---

[96] Evert, Walter: *"Aesthetics and Myth in the Poetry of Keats"*, Princeton: Princeton University Press, 1965, p.305.
[97] Bate, Walter Jackson: *"John Keats"*, Cambridge, Mass.: Harvard University Press, 1964.
[98] Sperry, Stuart: *"Keats the Poet"*, Princeton: Princeton University Press, 1973, p.288.
[99] Motion, Andrew: "Keats", London: Faber, 1997.

Although Keats was able to write a number of poems in 1819, he was in the grip of serious financial crisis throughout the year, constantly plagued by concerns over his brother, George, who, after emigrating to America, was badly in need of money. Despite these distractions, on 19 September 1819 he found time to write "*To Autumn*". The poem marks the final moment of his career as a poet. Hereafter, Keats's declining health and personal responsibilities began to raise obstacles to his continuing poetic efforts.

On 19 September 1819, Keats was walking near Winchester along the River Itchen. In a letter to his friend John Hamilton Reynolds written on 21 September, Keats described the impression the scenario had made upon him and its influence on the composition of his poem "*To Autumn*":

> *"How beautiful the season is now – How fine the air. A temperate sharpness about it [...] I never lik'd stubble fields so much as now [...] Somehow a stubble plain looks warm – in the same way that some pictures look warm – this struck me so much in my sunday's walk that I composed upon it."* [100]

'To Autumn'

Not everything on Keats's mind was quite clear at the time; the poet, however, knew in September that he would have to finally abandon '*Hyperion*'. Thus, in the letter that he wrote to Reynolds, Keats also included a note saying that

---

[100]. Keats, John: "*The Life and Letters of John Keats*", Ed. Richard Houghton (reprint). Read Books, 2008.

he abandoned his long poem.[101] Keats did not send "*To Autumn*" to Reynolds, but did include the poem within a letter to Richard Woodhouse, his publisher and friend, and dated it on the same day.[102]

> **"To Autumn"**
>
> "*Where are the songs of spring? Ay, Where are they?*
> *Think not of them, thou hast thy music too,—*
> *While barred clouds bloom the soft-dying day,*
> *And touch the stubble-plains with rosy hue;*
> *Then in a wailful choir the small gnats mourn*
> *Among the river sallows, borne aloft*
> *Or sinking as the light wind lives or dies;*
> *And full-grown lambs loud bleat from hilly bourn;*
> *Hedge-crickets sing; and now with treble soft*
> *The red-breast whistles from a garden-croft;*
> *And gathering swallows twitter in the skies.*"
>
> [John Keats, "*To Autumn*", lines 23---33]

The most striking aspect of *To Autumn* is that it inverts what happens in the *Ode on a Grecian Urn*. Keats paints visual images of autumn weaving a verbal tapestry, and by doing so transmutes the temporality inherent in the season into a spatial form like that of the urn.[103]

The poem "*To Autumn*" was revised and included in Keats's 1820 collection of poetry titled *Lamia, Isabella, the Eve of St. Agnes, and Other Poems*. Although the publishers Taylor and Hessey feared the kind of bad reviews that had plagued Keats's 1818 edition of *Endymion*, they were willing to publish the collection after the removal of any potentially controversial

---

[101] Bate, Walter Jackson: "*John Keats*", Cambridge, Mass.: Harvard University Press, 1964, p.585.

[102] Evert, Walter: "*Aesthetic and Myth in the Poetry of Keats*". Princeton: Princeton University Press, 1965, pp.296-297.

[103] Mirza, Shikoh Mohsin: "*Poetry of the Soul: The Sublime and Wondrous Odes of John Keats*", Wire, July 17, 2021. https://shorturl.at/lwBE6

poems to ensure that there would be no politically motivated reviews that could give the volume a bad reputation.[104]

Sketch of Keats by Charles Brown, August 1819, one month before the composition of "*To Autumn*"

The work "*To Autumn*" has been interpreted as a meditation on death; as an allegory of artistic creation; as Keats's response to the Peterloo Massacre, which took place in the same year; and as an expression of nationalist sentiment. One of the most anthologised English lyric poems, "*To Autumn*" has been regarded by critics as one of the most perfect short poems in the English language.

The subliminal

> ***"With a great poet the sense of Beauty overcomes every other consideration, or rather obliterates all consideration."***
>
> **-- John Keats**

By the time Keats came to write his odes, he had accepted the Greco-Roman thinker Longinus's idea that true art and literature always aspired towards spirituality and aesthetic grandeur, a quality that he called the

---

[104] McGann, Jerome: "*Keats and the Historical Method in Literary Criticism*", MLN 94 (1979), pp. 988–989.

'*Sublime*'. Longinus had identified the source of the *Sublime* as the inner being of the artist by writing in his treatise *On the Sublime* that "*Sublimity is the echo of greatness of soul*", essentially implying — what became the cornerstone of the Romantic aesthetics — that only pure and noble souls could produce great art.

From his writings, it transpires that as Keats wrote his odes he also added new aspects to the *Sublime*, aligning it with imagination, as Wordsworth had done in *The Prelude*. He discovered that it was the *Sublime* that enabled his poetic imagination to transform '*time into eternity*' and '*finite into infinite*'. Keats, therefore, relentlessly strived to achieve the *Sublime* in life and in poetry since he sensed that only this could help him to reach a stage of refined sensibility and heightened consciousness. As he was increasingly convinced that "*whatever the imagination seizes as Beauty must be Truth*", the urgent need of his Self to enfold and absorb the beauty of the physical world around him into the creative cosmos of his being became insistent and compelling.

This led Keats in his odes to eventually compose a kind of poetry that while mirroring his noble soul could at the same time embody the *Sublime* in its intellectual, ethical and spiritual dimensions.[105]

---

[105] Mirza, Shikoh Mohsin: "*Poetry of the Soul: The Sublime and Wondrous Odes of John Keats*", Wire, July 17, 2021. https://shorturl.at/lwBE6

Chapter 12
John Keats & Other Great English Romantic Poets of the 19th Century:

John Keats and Percy Bysshe Shelley

"For all their being yoked together in the minds of the public, the two [Keats & Shelley] are quite different poets, and were critical of one another's work"[106]

-- Mathew Sweeny

How close were Shelley and Keats?

Keats and Shelley were not as such bosom friends. They met each other a few times in 1817, before Shelley left England, but as fellow poet Leigh Hunt said: "*Keats did not take to Shelley as kindly as Shelley did to him.*" Initially at least, they were quite critical of each other's work. Their criticism of each other's work was, however, invariably with good intention, objective and in good taste, and none of them ever intended to unduly hurt the other.

After reading his first publication '*Endymion*', Shelly wrote to Keats in a bit critical manner saying, "*In poetry I have sought to avoid system and mannerism.*" Keats also, in a letter to Shelley, wrote somewhat tartly: "*You might curb your magnanimity, and be more of an artist, and load every rift of your subject with ore.*" In fine, as observed by the Irish poet Matthew Sweeney, despite "*all their being yoked together in the mind of the public, they were quite different poets and were critical of one another's work.*"

---

[106] "*How close were Shelley and Keats?*", The Irish Times, November 20, 2009.

December 1816: Keats meets Shelley

December 11, 1816.

Keats, aged twenty-one, meets the young, radical poet, Percy Bysshe Shelley, aged twenty-four, at Leigh Hunt's cottage in the Vale of Health, Hampstead. Hunt has just promoted Shelley and Keats as new '*Young Poets*', along with John Hamilton Reynolds, in a short essay in his paper, '*The Examiner*', dated December 1, 1816.

Shelley was by then already out there, with '*Queen Mab*', his "*Alastor*" volume, *Laon and Cythna*, and some fierce political pamphlets. Keats, on the other hand, had just two publications; first, a sonnet "*O Solitude*" published in *The Examiner*, back in May, 1816, while his second, namely, the sonnet "*On first looking into Chapman's Homer*" was also hosted by '*The Examiner*' in October the same year. Keats was thrilled; by then he had made up his mind to remain fully committed to poetry and to move away from a medical career.[107]

Keats visited Shelley again on his own on 15 February 1817, met him once again at Hunt's place in October, and thereafter, called on with Hunt in November.

As time rolled on, their friendship grew, but Keats never altogether warmed up to Shelley, though their closeness in age, general political beliefs, some common friends, and poetic aspirations might have joined the two more strongly. Reasons for their lack of a close friendship, some scholars believe, might have been due to class difference. Shelley was obviously aristocratic, while Keats despised rank; their dispositional differences also contributed to uneasy feelings, as did their wildly different lifestyles and fairly divergent ideas about the role of poetry, not to speak of an implicit rivalry between the two young poetic geniuses —who, with their divine potential, could write the best poetry one can imagine.

Like the Victorians, most others are fond of picturing Keats as delicate, frail, sickly and sensitive. True, he was short in stature; Keats was 5 feet 1 inch, while Shelley stood at almost 6 feet. Moreover, he did die of tuberculosis as did his brother Tom. But he was tough, a fighter at school,

---

[107] "*11 December 1816: Meeting Percy Shelley: Joined but not Close*", Mapping Keats's Progress: A Critical Chronology. . https://shorturl.at/ptSZ7

taking on the bullies. Unlike Shelley, who was a dreamy, nerdy kid at school, Keats was more of a troublemaker than a brainiac. He was known for his fierce prowess in schoolyard fights. As one student recalled, his classmates expected that he "*would become great - but rather in some military capacity than in literature.*"[108]

Joseph Severn: Posthumous Portrait of Shelley Writing "*Prometheus Unbound*" 1845

Most significantly, however, the two poets were characteristically so different. Unlike Keats, Shelley was polemical, highly political, scholarly, outwardly volatile, and fervently idealistic. Bullied and unhappy at Eton, he was already developing an independence of thought. His philosophical inclination would be further evident from a note added by Mary Shelley, his wife, to Shelley's mythical long poem "*Prometheus Unbound*". According to her, "*Shelley believed that mankind had only to will that there would be no evil, and there would be none.*" There is thus often a great sweep to his poetry, e.g., his "*Hymn to Intellectual Beauty*", which begins like this:

"*The awful shadow of some unseen Power*

Floats though unseen among us."

---

[108] "*Study Guide: John Keats Childhood*".
https://shorturl.at/stwLP

Likewise, his passionately indignant response to the Peterloo massacre of On August 16, 1819[109], *"The Mask of Anarchy"*, included the following lines very early on: *"I met Murder on the way"*

> ### *"The Mask of Anarchy" (1819)*
>
> *"As I lay asleep in Italy*
> *There came a voice from over the Sea*
> *And with great power it forth led me*
> *To walk in the visions of Poesy.*
> *I met Murder on the way -*
> *He had a mask like Castlereagh -*
> *Very smooth he looked, yet grim;*
> *Seven blood-hounds followed him:*
> *All were fat; and well they might*
> *Be in admirable plight,*
> *For one by one, and two by two,*
> *He tossed them human hearts to chew*
> *Which from his wide cloak he drew. […]"*
>
> [Percy B. Shelley, "The Mask of Anarchy"]

With the passage of time, it became apparent, at least to Hunt, that Shelley likes Keats more than Keats likes Shelley. But then, there is no denying the fact that they both were great poets and they both liked each other. Shelley liked him so much that he, of his own, invited Keats to stay with him at Pisa, when Keats, suffering from tuberculosis, was, on the advice of the doctors in

---

[109] The *"Peterloo Massacre"* took place on Monday 16 August 1819 at Manchester, Lancashire, England, Eighteen people died and 400-700 were injured when cavalry charged into a crowd of around 60,000 people who had gathered peacefully on Manchester's St Peter's Field. They came to appeal for adult suffrage and the reform of parliamentary representation. The disenfranchised working class—cotton workers, many of them women, with a large contingent of Irish workers—who made up the crowd were struggling with the increasingly dire economic conditions following the end of the Napoleonic Wars four years earlier.

London, was preparing to go to Italy to catch some sunshine and to avoid the English winter.

Keats, however, couldn't accept Shelley's invitation and chose to go to Rome as his doctor James Clark, the Scottish physician, who was to treat him in Italy, stayed in Rome. But he promised to Shelley that he would visit him in Pisa, which never happened for shortly after reaching Rome, he breathed his last on 23 February, 1821.

After Keats died in February 1821, Shelley composed a remarkable and classically-inspired pastoral elegy on Keats, "*Adonais*", in April, which was published in July that year. The elegy was patterned on Bion's lament for Adonais, and after showing the muses, the seasons, the dreams, the desires, the pleasures, and the sorrows - all weeping at the bier, rises "*to a triumphant declaration of the poet's immortality*".

The poem "*Adonais*" elevates Keats's status while also fashioning him as the sensitive victim of malevolent reviewers; this sticks to Keats's reputation well into the nineteenth century, though Shelley is not the first to sound the sentiment; in fact, it is right there on Keats's gravestone.

A year after, on 8 July, 1822, Shelley also died being drowned when his boat overturned off the Italian coast. He had been travelling back after visiting his friends, fellow Romantic poets, Lord Byron and James Leigh Hunt, to his home on the bay of Lerici in the north-west of the country. At the time of his death, Shelley was carrying in his pocket the manuscript of his "*The Indian Serenade*", the poems of Sophocles and of his dear friend -- John Keats.[110]

Keats and Shelley --- they are no more. They both died young in Italy, far away from England, their homeland, where their hearts truly belonged; and, till date they are remembered together. Today, more than two centuries after their death, they are still very much closely joined via the Keats-Shelley House in Rome (and its attendant Keats-Shelley Memorial Association), as well as the Keats-Shelley Association of America and its publication, "*The Keats-Shelley Review*".

----

[110] Schuster, M. Lincoln: "*The World's Great Letters*", Simon & Schuster Inc. New York City, New York, 1940, p.242.

Chapter 13
John Keats & Other Great English Romantic Poets of the 19th Century (Contd.):

John Keats and Lord George Gordon Byron

"You speak of Lord Byron and me – There is this great difference between us. He describes what he sees – I describe what I imagine – Mine is the hardest task."

-- John Keats, in a letter a letter to his brother George in September 1819

"Jack Keats or Ketch or whatever his names are."

-- Lord Byron to his publisher John Murray in a letter dated 4 November 1820

Early in her book about John Keats, Lucasta Miller calls Lord Byron an *"aristocratic megastar."*[111] Though not quite charitable, that funny epithet is perhaps appropriate for Byron's more-than-superstar celebrity in his day. Byron was the opposite of Keats. The rivalry and dislike between Byron and Keats has been much discussed; in their own time, however, it was felt far more keenly by Keats. In fact, just about three months before Keats's death, on 4 November 1820, Lord Byron from the Italian city of Ravenna wrote a letter to his publisher John Murray in London contemptuously

---

[111] Miller, Lucasta: *"Keats: A Brief Life in Nine Poems and One Epitaph"*, Vintage Digital, 4 February 2021.

referring to John Keats, a younger and much less well-known poet then, as "*Jack Keats or Ketch or whatever his names are.*" [112][113]

Earlier also, in December 1817, Byron did write a letter to Murray in which he had expressed his own unfavourable opinion about Keats's poetry. This letter is often cited as an example of Byron's contribution to the criticism Keats received from a section of critics particularly, from the *Quarterly Review* and *The Edinburgh Review*. In the letter, Byron famously referred to Keats's work as "*a sort of mental masturbation*" and criticized his use of language and style.

John Murray

Byron's letter and the *Quarterly Review*'s negative reviews had an impact on Keats' confidence and adversely acted upon Keats' reception in the literary community.

---

[112] Pinsky, Robert: "*A Poet's Poet: The Astonishing Career of John Keats*", The New York Times, April 15, 2022.

[113] "*Letter from Lord Byron to John Murray about the death of Keats, 26 April 1821*", Collection items, British Library. https://shorturl.at/lFWX9

Who killed John Keats? -- Excerpts from the Letter of Lord Byron to John Murray, July 30, 1821, shortly after the death of John Keats

After Keats died in February 1821, Shelley composed a remarkable and classically-inspired and Miltonic elegy on Keats, "*Adonais*", in April (published in July). Soon after the publication of '*Adonais*', Byron, in a letter dated July 30, 1821, wrote to Murray,[114]

> '*Are you aware that Shelley has written an elegy on Keats--and accuses the Quarterly of killing him?* [...]
>
> *Who killed John Keats?*
>
> *I, says the Quarterly*
>
> *So savage & Tartarly,*
>
> *'Twas one of my feats--*
>
> *Who shot the arrow?*
>
> *The poet-priest Milman*
>
> *(So ready to kill man)*
>
> *Or Southey, or Barrow.*—[115][116]

You know very well that I did not approve of Keats's poetry or principles of poetry--or of his abuse of Pope--but as he is dead--omit all that is said about him in any M.S.S. of mine--or publication. --His Hyperion is a fine monument & will keep his name--I do not envy the man--who wrote the article--your review people have no more right to kill than any other foot pads.--However--he who would die of an article in a review--would probably have died of something else

---

[114] Marchand, Leslie A.(ed.): "*Born for Opposition*": Byron's Letters and Journals, Vol. 8: 1821 London: John Murray, 1978.

[115] This parodies the nursery rhyme, "*Who killed Cock Robin?*"

[116] John Wilson Croker reviewed Keats' Endymion in the Quarterly Review in September 1818. Two other damning reviews joined Croker's, one by J. G. Lockhart in Blackwood's Edinburgh Magazine and another by an anonymous writer in British Critic. Keats died in Rome of consumption on February 23, 1821.

Milman: Henry Hart Milman (1791–1868), poet and dramatist; Southey: Robert Southey, the poet; Barrow: John Henry Barrow (1796–1858), journalist, editor, and man of letters

equally trivial--the same thing nearly happened to Kirke White--who afterwards died of consumption."

John Keats   Lord Byron

John Keats and Lord Byron -- both the poets belonged to the 19th century English Romantic movement, yet they were so vastly different that it is hard to imagine they were associated with the same genre. Byron was a tall, flamboyant and handsome nobleman whose wit, charm and ancestral title gave him access to the most elite circles of English society. He was also an accomplished and celebrated poet. His first major work, *"Childe Harold's Pilgrimage"* published between 1812 and 1818, was a great success and he enjoyed all the attendant benefits of celebrity. But, above all, he was a snob with so many privileges that he did not work hard to gain. Keats on the other hand, was a poor and struggling middle-class poet whose work was often subject to savage criticism by a powerful section of the critics of the age. He was advised that poetry was the provenance of nobleman such as Byron, and was dismissed (even by Byron, among others) as a *'Cockney'* poet. So, naturally there was a feeling of deprivation on his part vis-a-vis Byron's success. Neither liked the other's work, and both were very bitter about it.

Keats was just over five feet tall, and very sensitive about his stature. Upon reading a favourable review of his arch-rival Byron's work, he is said to have exclaimed: "*You see what it is to be six foot tall and a Lord*!"

Lord George Gordon Byron, 6th Baron Byron

Another reason for the ill-feeling between Byron and Keats was that the former revered the 18th century Augustan poets, particularly Alexander Pope, whose adherence to the classical tradition is echoed in his own early poetry. Keats's work was deeply at odds with the Augustans; also, his *"Sleep and Poetry"* (1816), which Byron read, was critical of their work. Keats found inspiration in the extravagant and sensuous wordplay of the 16th century and also admired the works of the first generation Romantic poets, such as, Wordsworth and Coleridge, who had caused a literary revolution with their rejection of Augustan classicism. And so, quite simply, Byron disliked Keats's poetry from an aesthetic standpoint.

Keats died of tuberculosis at the mere age of 25. Following his death, some of his friends, including Shelley, who wrote an elegy *"Adonais'* in memory of Keats, began to claim that his death had been hastened by the stress caused by uncharitable, vicious reviews of his work in the *Quarterly Review*. Byron found that hilarious, and, in poor taste, he even made fun of Keats, posthumously, in his famous narrative poem *"Don Juan"*:

"Don Juan" (1821)

> *"John Keats, who was killed off by one critique,*
> *Just as he really promised something great,*
> *If not intelligible, —without Greek,*
> *Contrived to talk about the Gods of late,*
> *Much as they might have been supposed to speak.*
> *Poor fellow! His was an untoward fate: —*
> *Tis strange the mind, that very fiery particle*
> *Should let itself be snuffed out by an article."*
>
> ["*Don Huan*", Canto XI, Stanza 60]

Shortly after the death of Keats, Byron wrote a letter dated 26 April 1821 from the Italian city of Ravenna to his publisher John Murray in London.[117] In the letter, Byron refers to the death of John Keats. Earlier he was out and out contemptuous in his remarks about Keats and had even said, "*Johnny Keats' piss a bed poetry*" as "*something like the pleasure an Italian fiddler extracted out of being suspended by a Street Walker in Drury Lane.*"[118] He was also of the view that Keats had taken '*the wrong line as a poet* – [and *he*] *was spoilt by Cockneyfying and Suburbing*'.[119]

---

[117] John Murray (27 November 1778 – 27 June 1843) was a Scottish publisher and member of the John Murray publishing house. He published works by authors such as Sir Walter Scott, Lord Byron, Jane Austen and Maria Rundell.

[118] This comment is said to have been made in private conversation with John Gibson Lockhart, a critic and writer of *Quarterly Review*, around 1817.

[119] The contrasting opinions expressed in the 16 April 1821 letter of Byron to Murray are interesting. Byron asks if Keats is dead because of John Wilson Croker's 1818 review from the Quarterly Review ('*a savage review is Hemlock to a sucking author*'), then states '*I am sorry for it*', inserting a '*very*' as an afterthought. Yet he goes on to be critical of the direction Keats's poetry took, and then describes how he (Byron) overcame the disappointment of a bad review, in a '*manly*' way – '*Instead of bursting a blood-vessel - I drank three bottles of claret - and began an answer*'. He states that he would not wish to have been responsible for the '*homicidal*' review of Keats's work and ends by returning to the dismissive tone by implying that Keats's poetry belonged to a '*School of Scribbling*'.

Keats felt likewise (though not so gross as Byron) about Byron's work; he considered it overrated, slavish and unoriginal. It was a sort of reverse snobbery. Prior to his death, Keats wrote a letter to his brother George in September 1819, wherein he addressed the differences between himself and Byron,

> *"You speak of Lord Byron and me – There is this great difference between us. He describes what he sees – I describe what I imagine – Mine is the hardest task."*

The rivalry between the two poets -- Keats and Byron – is thus quite apparent from the manner Keats wrote this letter; it is also clear that this rivalry was more acutely felt by Keats. Byron was a flamboyant and handsome nobleman whose wit, charm and ancestral title accorded him entry into the most elite circles of English society. John Keats, on the other hand, was a poor and struggling middle-class poet whose work was often savagely criticized by the prominent critics of the day.

It is hard to judge who was at fault for this feud and how it started, but it is apparent that despite being of a higher social class, it did not get reflected in the behaviour of Lord Byron, particularly in view of his unabashed gesture even after Keats death.

Chapter 14
Letters of John Keats (1816-21)

"His letters are what letters ought to be: the fine things come in unexpectedly, neither introduced nor shown out, but between trifle and trifle."

-- T.S. Eliot about John Keats

Keats died at an early age of twenty-five. Despite his short life span, he had perhaps the most remarkable career of any English poet; he published fifty-four poems, in three slim volumes and a few magazines. In his lifetime, he had very insignificant readership and was able to sell only 200 copies of his works. His genius was fully recognized long after his demise.

Poetry was clearly the dominant power and driving force behind Keats's short life. He writes passionately in his letters to his friends about his ambitions, about poetry and death, and his dedication to literary achievement. At one point he writes, "*I read and write about eight hours a day.*" and expresses his dedication to perfection when he states, "*…truth is I have been in such a state of Mind as to read over my Lines and hate them.*" On June 25-27, 1818, Keats writes to his brother:

> "*I shall learn poetry here and shall henceforth write more than ever, for the abstract endeavour of being able to add a mite to that mass of beauty which is harvested from these grand materials, by the finest spirits, and put into ethereal existence for the relish of one's fellows.*"

Keats was, as is apparent from his letter above, aware of his gift and strove very hard to perfect his talents in order to achieve and exude what it truly was to be, in his mind, an enlightened poet.

Apart from his poetry, over two hundred and forty letters written by Keats have survived over time. These letters synthesize his thoughts and philosophy, especially the letters he wrote to his brother George and his sister-in-law Georgiana, who had emigrated to the United States.

Many critics rank Keats's letters with his poems. According to American essayist, novelist and poet Christopher Morley,

> [These] letters as such form "*one of the few inexhaustible books in English literature […] the most thrilling and honorable reporting in our tongue, reporting the kind of things that people actually feel […]*".

Christopher Morley

"*His* [Keats's] *letters*," writes the American poet, essayist and playwright T.S. Eliot, "*are what letters ought to be: the fine things come in unexpectedly, neither introduced nor shown out, but between trifle and trifle.*" Together with his sonnets and odes, these letters form the true autobiography of John Keats.

T. S. Eliot

Indeed, if one reads Keats's letters, particularly the ones he wrote to the woman he loved, his muse Fanny Brawne -- one would see that perhaps even more than Keats's poetry, his letters to Fanny are what make him truly great as a genius.

The Importance of the Letters

Keats's letters begin in 1816 and end with his death in 1821. Apart from Fanny Brawne, his sweetheart, the recipients of the letters include his friends, namely, the poet John Hamilton Reynolds, and Benjamin Bailey, Keats's brothers George and Tom, his sister-in-law Georgiana, his sister Fanny Keats, his close associates, like, Leigh Hunt, Charles Brown, Percy Bysshe Shelley, as well as John Taylor and James Hessey, the London publishers who published his long poem *Endymion*.[120][121]

John Hamilton Reynolds

The excerpts from Keats's letters give us glimpses of his thoughts about poetry, and of the concerns that occupied him in 1817 and 1818, the years before he would write some of his best-known works, like, *Endymion, Isabella, The Eve of St. Agnes, Hyperion* etc. Together with his great works,

---

[120] *"Selections from Keats's Letters"*, Poetry Foundation.

[121] The letters of John Keats are full of mis-spellings. It is believed that Keats' mis-spellings are often indications of how his imagination was working, and are sometimes indications of an achieved suggestiveness which works within the poem itself. [See, Ricks, Christopher: *"Keats, Byron, and 'Slippery Blisses"*, Chapter IV in "Keats and Embarrassment", published by Oxford University Press. 1 March, 1984.]

his letters have also served generations of writers with provocative ideas and insights into poetry and the creative process. In the letters, he writes about some of the most noteworthy philosophical concepts, like, *beauty, the imagination*, and the concept of *"the Chameleon Poet," "the Vale of Soul-making," "the Mansion of Many Apartments."* and *"Negative Capability"*, a term he used for the first time in an 1817 letter. Keats also addresses the merits of other poets, including Milton, Keats's contemporary Wordsworth, and Shakespeare, whom Keats admired above all other writers. Such observations and imaginative spurts make Keats's letters essential reading for any poet or critic and as important as Keats's poems.

"Negative Capability"

"it struck me what quality went to form a Man of Achievement, especially in Literature, and which Shakespeare possessed so enormously - I mean Negative Capability, that is, when a man is capable of being in uncertainties, mysteries, doubts, without any irritable reaching after fact and reason."

— John Keats

"Negative Capability", is a concept first articulated by Keats in an 1817 letter about an artist's ability to access truth without the pressure and framework of logic or science. It is the writer's ability, which, according to Keats, *"Shakespeare possessed so enormously,"* to accept *"uncertainties, mysteries, doubts, without any irritable reaching after fact and reason."* An author possessing negative capability is objective and emotionally detached, as opposed to one who writes for didactic purposes; a literary work possessing negative capability may have beauties and depths that make conventional considerations of truth and morality irrelevant.[122]

"Chameleon Poet"

"What shocks the virtuous philosopher, delights the chameleon poet."

— John Keats

In a letter to Richard Woodhouse in October, 1818, Keats claims that the poet is a '*chameleon*'; according to him,

---

[122] Source: '*Encyclopedia Britannica*'.

"what shocks the virtuous philosopher, delights the camelion ["chameleon'] Poet. It does no harm from its relish of the dark side of things any more than from its taste for the bright one; because they both end in speculation. A Poet is the most unpoetical of anything in existence; because he has no Identity---he is continually in for---and filling some other Body---The Sun, the Moon, the Sea and Men and Women who are creatures of impulse are poetical and have about them an unchangeable attribute---the poet has none; no identity---he is certainly the most unpoetical of all God's Creatures. […]

It is a wretched thing to confess; but is a very fact that not one word I ever utter can be taken for granted as an opinion growing out of my identical nature---how can it, when I have no nature?"

"The Vale of Soul-Making"

"Call the world, if you please, "the Vale of Soul Making". Then you will find out the use of the world.

"[....] I can scarcely express what I but dimly perceive -- and yet I think I perceive it – […] I will call the world a school instituted for the purpose of teaching little children to read. I will call the human heart the hornbook used in that school. And I will call the child able to read, the soul made from that school and its hornbook."

-- John Keats

"*The Vale of Soul-Making*" is a concept introduced by the English Romantic poet John Keats in his letter to George and Tom Keats dated February 1819. This letter is often referred to as the "*Ode to Psyche*" letter because it reflects upon his thoughts in his own poem "*Ode to Psyche*", dedicated to the goddess Psyche from Greek mythology.

In this letter, Keats explores the idea that difficulties, challenges, and suffering in life contribute to the development and enrichment of the human soul. He uses the metaphor of a "Vale of Soul-Making" to describe the world as a place where the soul is shaped and refined through various experiences, both positive and negative. According to Keats, it is through these struggles and trials that human beings gain depth, wisdom, and a more profound understanding of themselves and the world around them.

In essence, Keats suggests that the challenges and difficulties faced by individuals are not to be seen as mere obstacles, but rather as opportunities for growth and transformation of the soul. This concept reflects Keats's own philosophical and poetic outlook, emphasizing the importance of embracing life's experiences, both positive and negative, as essential components of the human journey toward self-discovery and self-realization.

"Mansion of Many Apartments"

"I compare human life to a large Mansion of Many Apartments, two of which I can only describe, the doors of the rest being as yet shut upon me ---"

- John Keats

The concept of the "*Mansion of Many Apartments*" is another metaphorical idea put forth by Keats. This phrase appears in a letter he wrote to George and Tom Keats on September 21, 1819. In this letter, Keats uses the concept to convey his thoughts on the complexity of human experience, consciousness, and the layers of reality that individuals can access through imagination, poetry, and artistic expression.

According to Keats, for a great poet, imagination and creativity are central to his art, and his ability to tap into different layers of reality and experiences is more important than mere self-awareness or self-consciousness. The phrase "*Mansion of Many Apartments*" illustrates the multifaceted nature of consciousness and human experience. Each "apartment" represents a different realm of thought, emotion, perception, and understanding that a poet can explore and convey through their work.

Keats is suggesting that poets, or artists in general, have the unique ability to traverse various rooms (apartments) within the mansion of human consciousness. These rooms might include the intellectual, emotional, sensual, and imaginative spaces that contribute to the rich tapestry of human existence. By doing so, poets can capture the essence of life from diverse angles and perspectives, leading to a deeper and more holistic representation of reality. Furthermore, a poet's imaginative capacity allows him to transcend the limitations of self-awareness and enter into a realm where the boundaries between self and other, reality and imagination, are blurred. This enables poets to create works that resonate with a universal human experience, reaching beyond their own individuality.

In essence, the "*Mansion of Many Apartments*" concept speaks to the idea that a great poet's creative power lies in their ability to explore and express the diverse dimensions of human consciousness, going beyond mere self-consciousness and tapping into the universal and imaginative aspects of existence.

"Truth is Beauty"

> *"Beauty is truth, truth beauty, — that is all*
> *Ye know on earth, and all ye need to know."*
>
> **-- John Keats, '*Ode on a Grecian Urn*'**[123]

According to The Norton Anthology[124], this expression could also be known as *"beauty is reality"* or *"beauty is real"* which basically breaks down to the fact that beauty is all around us. And that is all one needs to recognise on this earth. The message Keats wishes to convey is that poetry is a mode of expression of beauty. In a letter to his brother George in 1819, he wrote, *"The great beauty of Poetry is, that it makes everything every place interesting."* A few years prior to the publication of *"Ode to "Grecian Urn,"* in 1819, Keats

---

[123] '*Ode on a Grecian Urn*' is about how great art transcends our own short, mortal lives. When Keats and his generation are all long dead, this Grecian urn will remain for future generations who experience similar woes to Keats, and the urn will be 'a friend to man', a consolation. After all, it has endured since the heyday of ancient Greece, over two millennia ago, until the time of Keats himself, in the early nineteenth century.

In the last two lines of '*Ode on a Grecian Urn*', the urn 'speaks', as Keats sums up the message of this timeless work of art as:

> '*Beauty is truth, truth beauty, — that is all*
> *Ye know on earth, and all ye need to know.*'

In other words, beauty is all we need in order to discover truth, and truth is itself beautiful. This is all we, are mere mortals, know, but it's all we need to know: we shouldn't impatiently go in pursuit of answers which we don't need to have. Implied in these last lines of Keats's poem is the suggestion that we shouldn't attempt to find concrete answers to everything; sometimes the mystery is enough. [Source: Tearle, Oliver: *"The True Meaning of Keats's 'Beauty is Truth, Truth Beauty'"*, Interesting Literature.]

[124] The Norton Anthology of English Literature is an anthology of English literature published by W. W. Norton & Company. First published in 1962, it has gone through ten editions; as of 2006 there are over eight million copies in print, making it the publisher's best-selling anthology. M. H. Abrams, a critic and scholar of Romanticism, served as General Editor for its first seven editions, before handing the job to Stephen Greenblatt, a Shakespeare scholar and Harvard professor. The anthology provides an overview of poetry, drama, prose fiction, essays, and letters from Beowulf to the beginning of the 21st century. [Source: *Wikipedia*]

wrote a letter to Benjamin Bailey (1817) which documented the beginning of the beauty/truth theology, *"What the imagination seizes as Beauty must be truth."*

If beauty is truth, it raises a good question. What is beauty? It is no definitive thing. We might be able to find examples of beauty, but beauty itself is merely a concept. This concept is truthful to each human, individually. This transcendent view of beauty is something that marked the Romantic period of British literature.

Keats's contemporaries wrote specific essays and prefaces in defence of poetry, but Keats did not. He is known for the luxurious and sensational quality of his poems. These works of *"art for art's sake"* leave an impression of a young sensual poet who lacks depth. When his biography was published almost thirty years after his death, his letters revealed the depth to which he had thought about poetry and life. Norton claimed that Keats explored every seed of thought that he and his friends Cole and Hazlitt discussed, and that he was always pursuing new meaning.

Genius: T.S. Eliot

"The only means of strengthening one's intellect is to make up one's mind about nothing -- to let the mind be a thoroughfare for all thoughts.

-- **John Keats**

T. S. Eliot believed Keats's judgment of poetry to be *"genius"* for a man so young. His *'philosophic mind'* allowed him to shed his ego and *"let the mind be a thoroughfare for all thoughts."* Walter Jackson Bate believed that this saved him from not having to reject any thought that cannot be *"wrenched into a ...systematic structure of one's own making"*. Lionel Trilling was of the view that in Keats *"we have the wisdom of maturity arising from the preoccupations of youth."* Keats spent his short life discussing and pursuing the *"burden of the mystery.'*[125]

---

[125] Spivey Nicole, Uffelman Lindsay, Keeports Katie, Grewal Ann: *"Keats's Letters"*, British Literature Wiki.

Chapter 15
Keats & Fanny Brawne: Love unbounded

"I don't need the stars in the night I found my treasure
All I need is you by my side so shine forever."

-- John Keats

Between September and November 1818: Keats meets Fanny

It was an unusually cold English winter. The month had begun badly, with a portent of worse to come. Brown's maid had told him that Keats was taking laudanum (opium)[126]; when confronted, Keats promised to stop. But while Brown believed Keats took it '*to keep up his spirits*', the truth was that he used it as a normal pain-killer. The occasional sore throat and cough which had troubled him was still dismissed as a mere cold, but a new tightness in his chest had begun.

On February 3, 1820, Keats had gone into the city of London to visit friends and *"returned late"*. As it was cheapest to ride outside the stagecoach, he did so, but he lacked a warm coat and the night was bitterly cold and windy. He arrived at **his friend Brown's house** in a *"cold and feverish"* state. He staggered so badly that Brown initially thought he was drunk. But soon he realized Keats was ill and sent him upstairs to bed. Brown then brought him a glass of spirits. As he entered the room, he heard Keats cough. It was just a slight cough, but Keats said: *"That is blood from my mouth"*. There was a drop of blood upon his bed sheet. He said to Brown, *"Bring me the candle, Brown, and let me see this blood"*. Both men looked upon it for a moment; then Keats looked up at his friend calmly and nodded his head in despair. As one who had studied medicine, he knew what was coming. He was only too familiar with it; his mother had died of consumption. Only a year ago, his

---

[126] In the early 16th century, Paracelsus made an opium pill (it also contained citrus juice and gold) and a tincture (alcohol extract) of opium called '*laudanum*' (from the Latin laudare, to praise) for pain relief, which is still available in some countries. Taken in high doses, it can even cause death

brother Tom, whom he nursed devotedly, also died of it. Now it was his turn; he said to Brown, *"I know the colour of that blood; it is arterial blood. I cannot be deceived in that colour. That drop of blood is my death warrant. I must die."*

Later that night, a large lung haemorrhage followed that almost suffocated him. Keats knew his end was near. All he could think of was 'Fanny', *"the beautiful, graceful, silly, fashionable and strange"* girl he had fallen in love for a little over a year ago, with whom he had a *"little tiff now and then"*. Fanny seldom visited Keats in person over the next month for fear of his delicate health giving out, but occasionally would pass by his window after walks, and the two often wrote notes to each other.[127][128]

Letters and drafts of poems suggest that Keats first met Frances (Fanny) Brawne between September and November 1818. They met at *"Wentworth Place"*, a block of two houses, white-stuccoed and semi-detached, built by Charles Brown and Charles Dilke -- now the *"Keats House"* Museum, Hampstead, where the poet had been living for some time with his friend Brown.[129]

Keats and Fanny: Love at first sight

"You cannot conceive how I ache to be with you:
how I would die for one hour..."

-- **John Keats**

It was autumn of 1818. Keats had recently returned from a walking tour of Scotland with his friend Charles Brown. Brown had rented out his portion of the double house called *"Wentworth Place"* to the Brawne family for the summer. When they returned, the Brawnes moved to Elm Cottage, a brief walk away. But while they lived at Wentworth Place, they had become close friends with Brown's neighbours (and Keats's friends), the Dilke family. The Dilkes were fond of Keats and had spoken of him to the Brawnes often,

---

[127] Brown, Charles Armitage (edited by Dorothy Hyde Bodurtha and W. B. Pope): *"Life of John Keats"*, Oxford University Press, 1937.
[128] Rollins, Hyder E.: *"The Keats Circle: Letters and Papers 1816-78"*, ed. Hyder E. Rollins Harvard, 2nd edition, 1965.
[129] Gittings, Robert: *"John Keats"*, London: Heinemann, 1968.

praising him in the highest terms. And so when the Brawne family finally met young Keats, they were prepared to like him.

Fanny Brawne, the elder daughter of the Brawn family, was born on August 9, 1800 near Hampstead. After her father died in 1810, Fanny, her mother, and her two younger siblings lived in a series of rented houses. Throughout her youth, she was interested in fashion, was an expert on historical costume, and was skilled at sewing, knitting and embroidery. **Keats and Fanny met at Wentworth Place in October or November 1818.**

Keats fell in love with Fanny when he saw her walking in her garden. It was love at first sight; he initially considered her a 'minx' but could not help falling in love with her.

"Shall I give you Miss Brawn[e]?" : Keats writes to his brother and sister-in-law in a letter dated December 25, 1818

Soon after first meeting Brawne (and confessing he found her both beautiful and strange), Keats wrote to his brother George and his sister-in-law Georgiana, in a letter dated December 25, 1818:[130]

"Shall I give you Miss Brawn[e]*?"*

"Shall I give you Miss Brawn[e]*?* "*She is about my height–with a fine style of countenance of the lengthened sort – she wants sentiment in every feature – she manages to make her hair look well – her nostrils are fine – though a little painful – her mouth is both bad and good –her Profile is better than her full-face which indeed is not full but pale and thin without showing any bone. Her shape is very graceful and so are her movements – her Arms are good her hands baddish – her feet tolerable. She is not seventeen – but she is ignorant – monstrous in her behaviour, flying out in all directions, calling people such names that I was forced lately to make use of the term Minx – this I think not from any innate vice, but from a penchant she has for acting stylishly. I am however tired of such style and shall decline any more of it."*

---

[130] Keats, John: *"The complete poetical works and letters of John Keats"*, Cambridge Edition, Boston and New York, Houghton, Mifflin and Company, The University Press, Cambridge, 1899, pp. 342-343.

Fanny had blue eyes and would often wear blue ribbons in her brown hair *"Her mouth expressed determination and a sense of humour and her smile was disarming. She knew the value of elegance; velvet hats and muslin bonnets, crepe hats with argus feathers, straw hats embellished with grapes and tartan ribbons[...] She could answer, at a moment's notice, any question on historical costume. ... Fanny enjoyed music...[and] was fiery in discussion; she was a voluminous reader. ... Indeed, books were her favourite topic of conversation"*. She also had a talent for dress-making and languages as well as a natural theatrical bent.

The relationship between Keats and Fanny started off well and was cordial. Fanny enjoyed his company, recalling that *"his conversation was in the highest degree interesting and his spirits good, excepting at moments when anxiety regarding his brother's health dejected them"*.[131]

During November 1818, Fanny developed an intimacy with Keats, but it was shadowed by the illness of his younger brother Tom, whom he was nursing through this period.

On 1 December 1818, Tom died of tuberculosis, at age nineteen. Keats's grief was deep; the memory of Tom's terrible, lingering illness was too dreadful for him to forget. After Tom's death, Keats was eager to escape. Well Walk, once the scene of close companionship for the Keats brothers, now haunted him with disappointment, despair and grief. So he gladly accepted Brown's invitation to share Wentworth Place with him. Keats paid him the normal rate for lodging. Since he now lived close to the Brawnes, he would meet Fanny more frequently; and each time, the brown haired, blue-eyed Fanny made a greater impression on him. She both confused and exasperated Keats. He simply could not understand her. Enigmatic though she seemed to be, **Fanny** was a welcome distraction **and** she gave him sympathy, keeping his mind from the past and from introspection; she revitalized Keats with her vivacity and love.

Keats on a creative spree – with Fanny as his muse

"I have met with women who I really think would like to be married to a Poem and to be given away by a Novel".

-- **John Keats**

---

[131] Richardson, Joanna. *"Fanny Brawne: A Biography"*, Norwich: Jarrold and Sons, 1952.

Keats fell completely in love with Fanny. Poetry was his passion. But it was only a matter of time before both Fanny and poetry occupied positions of equal importance in his life. Keats had once remarked, *"I have met with women who I really think would like to be married to a Poem and to be given away by a Novel"*. But now with Fanny in his life, the world seemed to have changed. He was on a creative spree; she was his muse –she read his work, admired it, and inspired him to write some of his greatest literary works.

On 3 April 1819, the Dilkes moved to the city centre and rented their half of Wentworth Place to the Brawne family. Fanny was now a next-door neighbour of Keats. Their proximity was intoxicating for Keats. From April onward, the romance between Keats and Fanny blossomed. Keats began to lend Brawne books, such as Dante's *"Inferno"*, and they would read together. He gave her the love sonnet *"Bright Star"* as a declaration of his love. It was a work in progress which he continued at until the last months of his life, and the poem came to be reckoned as an immortal testimony of their relationship.

When they first met, Keats was struck by her coquettish sense of fun. Hampstead, where she lived, was close to an army barrack; so there were numerous military dances throughout the year. Fanny loved to dance; she was a popular participant in these parties. It was not quite to the liking of Keats as it would make him jealous. *"My greatest torment since I have known you has been the fear of you being a little inclined to the Cressid,"* he would tell her later, referring to Chaucer's infamous flirt.

Brown was not happy about their relationship (it may also be due to jealousy on his part). As a close friend and well-wisher of Keats, he disliked Fanny for she consumed much of Keats's time. To him, Fanny's casual, flirtatious attitude towards other men, including to Brown himself, seemed to be too shallow to match the depth of Keats's feelings and attraction towards her. He was averse to her teasing behaviour and the depression and jealousy it aroused in Keats. Distracted by such antics, how could Keats write?

But Brown's apprehension was misplaced. Keats's intense passion and love for Fanny gave him new impetus – new inspiration – new insight into his own emotions and the world itself. His poetry began to reflect new maturity and power. It all led to the beginning of Keats's *'annus mirabilis'* — the yearlong spell of creative vitality under which he produced most of his masterpieces, including his *"Ode to a Nightingale."*

Keats wrote numerous love letters to Fanny Brawne – which are among the most famous love letters ever written. They exchanged several short notes, and occasionally more passionate ones. None of Fanny's letters to Keats survive. From this, however, it seems he was often unsettled by her behaviour and uncertain of her affection. His illness brought them closer; when he left for Rome, they were engaged and deeply in love.

Keats's love letters **were first published in instalments between 1848 and 1878.**The letters shocked the literary circle of the Victorian England in the nineteenth century. Men like Matthew Arnold and Algernon Swinburne stated that they were too emotional, and should not be presented to public view. Today, Keats's love letters are acknowledged to be among the greatest of their kind and is a timelessly enchanting read as matchless instances of expressions of love --- and to some of these, we may now turn.

Chapter 16
Love Letters of John Keats

"And when thou art weary I'll find thee a bed,
Of mosses and flowers to pillow thy head."

-- John Keats, 'To Emma'[132]

In the summer of 1819, Keats went to the Isle of Wight and thence to Margate that he might study and write undisturbed. While he was staying at Shanklin in the beautiful Isle of Wight, Keats wrote his first letter to Fanny:[133]

July 3, 1819

"I almost wish we were butterflies and liv'd but three summer days"

"*Shanklin, Isle of Wight, Thursday*

[Postmark: Newport, July 3, 1819]

MY DEAREST LADY

I am glad I had not an opportunity of sending off a Letter which I wrote for you on Tuesday night— 'twas too much like one out of Rousseau's Heloise. I am more reasonable this morning. The morning is the only proper time for me to write to a beautiful Girl whom I love so much: for at night, when the lonely day has closed, and the lonely, silent, unmusical Chamber is waiting to receive me as into a Sepulchre, then believe me my passion gets entirely the sway, then I would not have you see those Rhapsodies which I once thought it impossible I should ever

---

[132] Written probably in 1815. Keats's brother George copied this poem and addressed it to his later wife, Georgiana Wylie. First published in 1883.
[133] Keats, John: "*The complete poetical works and letters of John Keats*", Cambridge Edition, Boston and New York, Houghton, Mifflin and Company, The University Press, Cambridge, 1899, pp. 380-381.

give way to, and which I have often laughed at in another, for fear you should [think me] either too unhappy or perhaps a little mad.

I am now at a very pleasant Cottage window, looking onto a beautiful hilly country, with a glimpse of the sea; the morning is very fine. I do not know how elastic my spirit might be, what pleasure I might have in living here and breathing and wandering as free as a stag about this beautiful Coast if the remembrance of you did not weigh so upon me I have never known any unalloy'd Happiness for many days together: the death or sickness of someone has always spoilt my hours, and now when none such troubles oppress me, it is you must confess very hard that another sort of pain should haunt me.

Ask yourself my love whether you are not very cruel to have so entrammelled me, so destroyed my freedom. Will you confess this in the Letter you must write immediately, and do all you can to console me in it—make it rich as a draught of poppies to intoxicate me—write the softest words and kiss them that I may at least touch my lips where yours have been. For myself I know not how to express my devotion to so fair a form: I want a brighter word than bright, a fairer word than fair. I almost wish we were butterflies and liv'd but three summer days—three such days with you I could fill with more delight than fifty common years could ever contain. But however selfish I may feel, I am sure I could never act selfishly: as I told you a day or two before I left Hampstead, I will never return to London if my Fate does not turn up Pam or at least a Court-card. Though I could centre my Happiness in you, I cannot expect to engross your heart so entirely, indeed if I thought you felt as much for me as I do for you at this moment I do not think I could restrain myself from seeing you again tomorrow for the delight of one embrace.

But no, I must live upon hope and Chance. In case of the worst that can happen, I shall still love you, but what hatred shall I have for another!

Some lines I read the other day are continually ringing a peal in my ears:

To see those eyes I prize above mine own

Dart favors on another—

And those sweet lips (yielding immortal nectar)

Be gently press'd by any but myself—

Think, think Francesca, what a cursed thing

It were beyond express

J. KEATS

Do write immediately. There is no Post from this Place, so you must address Post Office, Newport, Isle of Wight. I know before night I shall curse myself for having sent you so cold a Letter; yet it is better to do it as much in my senses as possible. Be as kind as the distance will permit to your ...

Present my Compliments to your mother, my love to Margaret and best remembrances to your Brother, if you please so."

A sketch of Keats cottage at the Isle of Wight,
Keats House Museum, Hampstead

October 1819: Keats returns to Hampstead & meets Fanny after three months' absence: "you dazzled me"

-- **John Keats to Fanny Brawne**

In August, Keats left the Isle of Wight for Winchester. Here he wrote the second part of *"Lamia"* and the beautiful *"To Autumn"*. He returned to Hampstead in October. Their meeting after his three months' absence overwhelmed Keats; *"you dazzled me"*, he wrote to Fanny. She was still a tease and deliberately stoked his jealousy. The poet remained torn between his work and his love; but it only spurred his creative genius.

As days passed, Keats's love for Fanny became more and more intense. As his illness progressed, his emotional craving focused more and more on his nineteen-year-old Hampstead neighbour, Fanny Brawne. He wanted to live and enjoy his love. But it was becoming increasingly clear to him that his end was not too far. It was only his love for Fanny that still helped him keep going and enjoy the beauty of life and the world around. So, even when he would write to her of his literary legacy, he sounded more resigned than bitter: *"I have left no immortal work behind me—nothing to make my friends proud of my memory—but I have lov'd the principle of beauty in all things, and if I had had time I would have made myself remember'd."*

Keats: uncomfortable with women and hoped he'll never marry

July 18, 1818": "I have not a right feeling towards women"

Before Fanny came into his life, Keats was one who felt uncomfortable with women. In a letter dated July 18, 1818 (just a few months before he met Fanny) addressed to his friend Benjamin Bailey, he wrote:[134][135]

---

[134] Benjamin Bailey (1791-1853) was a student at Oxford when he and Keats became friends. The friendship ended when Bailey, after passionately courting Marianne Reynolds, married Hamilton Gleig instead. The marriage may have been determined by his career; Gleig was the daughter of the bishop of Brechin and Bailey was a country parson. Keats's last letter to Bailey was an achingly polite congratulations on his wedding. [See, Hanson, Marilee. *"John Keats Letter To Benjamin Bailey, 10 June 1818"*, English History, March 17, 2015]

[135] Keats, John: *"The complete poetical works and letters of John Keats"*, Cambridge Edition, Boston and New York, Houghton, Mifflin and Company, The University Press, Cambridge, 1899, pp. 318-319.

Benjamin Bailey

"Inverary, July 18 [1818]

My Dear Bailey,

"[...] I am certain I have not a right feeling towards women--at this moment I am striving to be just to them but I cannot--Is it because they fall so far beneath my boyish imagination? When I was a Schoolboy I thought a fair woman a pure Goddess, my mind was a soft nest in which some one of them slept though she knew it not--I have no right to expect more than their reality. I thought them ethereal above Men--I find them perhaps equal — great by comparison is very small. Insult may be inflicted in more ways than by word or action — One who is tender of being insulted does not like to think an insult against another. I do not like to think insults in a lady's company — I commit a crime with her which absence would not have known. Is it not extraordinary? When among Men I have no evil thoughts, no malice, no spleen – I can listen and from every one I can learn – my hands are in my pockets I am free from all suspicion and comfortable. When I am among women I have evil thoughts, malice, spleen – I cannot speak or be silent – I am full of suspicions and therefore listen to nothing – I am in a hurry to be gone. You must be charitable and put all this perversity to my being disappointed

since my boyhood. With all this, trust me, I have not the least idea that men of different feelings and inclinations are more short-sighted than myself. I never rejoiced more than at my Brother's marriage, and shall do so at that of any of my friends. I must absolutely get over this — but how? the only way is to find the root of the evil, and so cure it "with backward mutters of dissevering power"— that is a difficult thing; for an obstinate Prejudice can seldom be produced but from a Gordian complication of feelings, which must take time to unravel, and care to keep unravelled. I could say a good deal about this, but I will leave it, in hopes of better and more worthy dispositions — and also content that I am wronging no one, for after all I do think better of womankind than to suppose they care whether Mister John Keats five feet high likes them or not."

Your affectionate Friend,

JOHN KEATS."

October 25, 1818: "...I hope I shall never marry."

Keats had even professed not to marry, preferring solitude, the life of imagination, and appreciation of beauty. In a letter dated October 25, 1818 to his brother George and his sister-in-law Georgiana, he gave a vivid picture of the way he intended to pass his life. He wrote:[136]

> ".. I shall in a short time write you as far as I know how I intend to pass my life – I cannot think of the things now.
>
> Tom is so unwell and weak. Notwithstand[ing] your Happiness and your recommendation I hope I shall never marry. Though the most beautiful Creature were waiting for me at the end of a Journey or a walk; though the carpet were of Silk, the Curtains of the morning Clouds; the chairs and Sofa stuffed with Cygnet's down; the food Manna, the Wine beyond Claret, the Window opening on Winandermere, I should not feel--or rather my Happiness would not

---

[136] Keats, John: "*The complete poetical works and letters of John Keats*", Cambridge Edition, Boston and New York, Houghton, Mifflin and Company, The University Press, Cambridge, 1899, pp. 334-335.

be so fine, as my Solitude is sublime. ...The roaring of the wind is my wife and the Stars through the windowpane are my Children. The mighty abstract Idea I have of Beauty in all things stifles the more divided and minute domestic happiness--an amiable wife and sweet Children I contemplate as a part of that Beauty, but I must have a thousand of those beautiful particles to fill up my heart. I feel more and more every day, as my imagination strengthens, that I do not live in this world alone but in a thousand worlds--No sooner am I alone than shapes of epic greatness are stationed around me, and serve my Spirit the office which is equivalent to a King's body guard -- then "Tragedy with scepter'd pall comes sweeping by." According to my state of mind I am with Achilles shouting in the Trenches or with Theocritus in the Vales of Sicily. Or I throw my whole being into Troilus, and repeating those lines, "I wander like a lost Soul upon the stygian Banks staying for waftage", I melt into the air with a voluptuousness so delicate that I am content to be alone. These things, combined with the opinion I have of the generality of women - who appear to me as children to whom I would rather give a sugar plum than my time, form a barrier against Matrimony which I rejoice in. I have written this that you might see I have my share of the highest pleasures and that though I may choose to pass my days alone I shall be no Solitary... I am as happy as a Man can be... with the yearning Passion I have for the beautiful, connected and made one with the ambition of my intellect..."

Your anxious and affectionate Brother

JOHN."

Tom died five weeks later on December 1, 1818. The bereavement intensified Keats's desire for communion with solitude; but fortunately for the world of literature, he channelled it as a creative force, immersing himself ever more deeply into that great resource within his own breast. At about the same time, in November 1818, Fanny came into his life and it was not long before Keats developed an uncanny obsession for her.

It may seem somewhat strange that not long after John Keats extolled the joys of being single, he fell in love. It is strange that despite having so strong sentiments towards women and marriage, Keats developed such intense attraction and obsession for Fanny's love – that too within such a short time. Some scholars are of the opinion perhaps it grew out of Keats's feeling that Fanny was his equal. In his biography of John Keats[137], R. S. White has observed *"Perhaps the main aspect of the relationship lies in the fact that Keats seems able from the start to speak to Fanny without the kind of crippling self-consciousness or tongue-tied self-annulment he felt in the presence of other women"*. This feeling of being on a more equal footing with Fanny was somewhat unusual for Keats as he generally found talking to and interacting with women to be troublesome and tedious. But it may well be that Keats's poetic effusion found its ultimate voice and expression in Fanny and there lies the genesis of his intense love and passion for her. The Fanny he loved was the creation of his imagination, his passion. She was the beauty which for him became the truth; she was for him the fulfilment of *'Endymion'*, the very symbol of beauty, the reconciliation between real life and his poetic quest.

Whether such obsessive love as Keats had for Fanny is wise is an issue that has engaged the attention of many scholars. In the opinion of the 19th century American poet and critic R. H. Stoddard:

> *"I know of nothing comparable with them in English literature – know nothing that is so unselfish, so longing, so adoring – nothing that is so mad, so pitiful, so utterly weak and wretched. John Keats was a great genius, but he had not one particle of common-sense – for himself. Few men of genius ever do have… Why, a boy might have told Keats that the way to woo and win a woman was not to bare his heart before her, as he did before Fanny Brawne, and not to let her know, as he did, that he was her captive. If he had had the least glimmer of common-sense, he never would have surrendered at discretion."*

Keats's letters to Fanny are among the most famous love letters ever written. As next door neighbours, they exchanged numerous short notes, and occasionally more passionate ones. None of Fanny's letters to Keats survive. From his, however, it seems he was often unsettled by her behaviour and uncertain of her affection. His illness brought them closer; when he left for Rome, they were engaged and deeply in love.

---

[137] White, R.S. *"John Keats: A Literary Life"*. Palgrave Macmillan, 2010, p.146.

October 13, 1819: Keats to Fanny: "Love is my religion"

They came to know each other around November 1818. Within months, they were deeply in love. In a letter dated October 13, 1819 to Fanny, Keats wrote,[138] *"I have been astonished that Men could die Martyrs for religion – I have shudder'd at it – I shudder no more –I could be martyr'd for my Religion – Love is my religion – I could die for that – I could die for you."*

[Postmark: October 13, 1819]

"25 College Street

MY DEAREST GIRL,

This moment I have set myself to copy some verses out fair. I cannot proceed with any degree of content. I must write you a line or two and see if that will assist in dismissing you from my Mind for ever so short a time. Upon my Soul I can think of nothing else – The time is passed when I had power to advise and warn you again[s]t the unpromising morning of my Life – My love has made me selfish. I cannot exist without you – I am forgetful of everything but seeing you again – my life seems to stop there – I see no further. You have absorb'd me.... I have no limit now to my love – ... I have been astonished that Men could die Martyrs for religion – I have shudder'd at it – I shudder no more – I could be martyr'd for my Religion – Love is my religion – I could die for that – I could die for you. My Creed is Love and you are its only tenet – You have ravish'd me away by a power I cannot resist: and yet I could resist till I saw you; and even since I have seen you I have endeavoured often "to reason against the reasons of my Love." I can do that no more – the pain would be too great – My love is selfish – I cannot breathe without you.

Yours for ever

JOHN KEATS."

---

[138] Keats, John: *"The complete poetical works and letters of John Keats"*, Cambridge Edition, Boston and New York, Houghton, Mifflin and Company, The University Press, Cambridge, 1899, pp. 413-414.

Five days later, on October 18, 1819 Keats proposed to Fanny, and they were engaged. As a token of love, he gave her in 1820 a gold engagement ring set with an almandine stone – a dark mineral believed to have power of healing and protection -- with a reddish violet hue. Though a significant event in their lives, they did their best to keep their engagement a secret.

Fanny Brawne's engagement ring,
Keats House Museum, Hampstead

The engagement ring Keats gave to Fanny is currently on display in the "Keats House" Museum, Keats Grove, Hampstead, London.

Chapter 17
More Love Letters of John Keats (1820)

"I have so much of you in my heart."

-- John Keats

In the very beginning of the first week of February, 1820, Keats had pulmonary haemorrhage, which, according to Charles Brown, signalled that he would possibly not recover from his illness. Thereafter, he would be confined to his room in Wentworth Place for much of the next month. Meanwhile, Fanny was living just on the other side of a wall from Keats. Because of his condition, and out of fear of passing his disease to Fanny, Keats primarily communicated to her via short messages written on small pieces of paper and delivered by hand to the other side of the house.

In the first of these approximately 15 letters from February 1820, which comes just one day after Keats's pulmonary haemorrhage, Keats sounds a somewhat optimistic note, predicting that while the doctors were saying he "*must remain confined to this room for some time,*" it would nonetheless be a "*pleasant prison*" because of Fanny's presence: "T*he consciousness that you love me will make a pleasant prison of the house next to yours.*"

Text of the letter can be accessed via the original form in which it was first published: Forman's 1878 "*Letters of John Keats to Fanny Brawne*". The letter is undated in that edition, but Forman estimates the date as 4 February in later editions, and as do other editors.[139]

4 (?) February, 1820: "The consciousness that you love me will make a pleasant prison of the house next to yours."

"*Dearest Fanny,*

---

[139] "*Letter #183: To Fanny Brawne, 4 (?) Feb 1820*", The Keats Letters Project, February 4, 2020. https://shorturl.at/fiJZ5

I shall send this the moment you return. They say I must remain confined to this room for some time. The consciousness that you love me will make a pleasant prison of the house next to yours. You must come and see me frequently: this evening without fail --- when you must not mind about my speaking in a low tone for I am ordered to do so though I can speak out.

Yours ever

Sweetest love, ---

J. Keats

turn over

Perhaps your mother is not at home and so you must wait till she comes. You must see me tonight and let me hear you promise to come tomorrow.

Brown told me you were all out. I have been looking for the stage the whole afternoon. Had I known this I could not have remain'd so silent all day."

However, with the passage of time, the prison apparently became less and less pleasant to him. It is not difficult to imagine the kind of torment that was posed by the combination of nearness and absence that this situation enforced on the young couple.

The following are just a few from among the many letters Keats wrote to Fanny in 1820 as his health was deteriorating day by day.

10 (?) February 1820: "You had a just right to be a little silent to one who speaks so plainly to you."

My dearest Girl –

If illness makes such an agreeable variety in the manner of your eyes I should wish you sometimes to be ill. I wish I had read your note before you went last night that I might have assured you how far I was from suspecting any coldness: You had a just right to be a little silent to one who speaks so plainly to you. You must believe you shall, you will that I can do nothing say nothing think nothing of you but what has its spring in the Love which has so long been my pleasure and torment. On the night I was taken ill when so violent a rush of blood came to my Lungs that I felt nearly suffocated – I assure you I felt it possible I might not survive and at that moment thought[t] of nothing but you – When I said to Brown 'this is unfortunate' I thought of you – 'T is true that since the first two or three days other subjects have entered my head – I shall be looking forward to Health and the Spring and a regular routine of our old Walks.

Your affectionate

John Keats

(?) February 1820: "I read your note in bed last night, and that might be the reason of my sleeping so much better."

My dearest Fanny,

I read your note in bed last night, and that might be the reason of my sleeping so much better. I think Mr Brown is right in supposing you may stop too long with me, so very nervous as I am. Send me every evening a written Good night. If you come for a few minutes about six it may be the best time. Should you ever fancy me too low-spirited I must warn you to ascbribe [for ascribe] it to the medicine I am at present taking which is of a nerve-shaking nature – I shall impute any depression I may experience to this cause. I have been writing with a vile old pen the whole week, which is excessively ungallant. The fault is in the Quill: I have mended it and still it is very much inclin'd to make blind es. However these last lines are in a much better style of penmanship thof [for though] a little disfigured by the smear of black currant jelly; which has made a little mark on one of the Pages of Brown's Ben Jonson, the very best book he has. I have lick'd it but it remains very purple [for purple]. I did not know whether to say purple or blue, so in the mixture of the thought wrote purplue which may be an excellent name for a colour made up of those two, and would suit well to start next spring. Be very careful of open doors and windows and going without your duffle grey God bless you Love! –

J. Keats-

P.S. I am sitting in the back room – Remember me to your Mother.

***(?) March, 1820**: "Even if you did not love me I could not help an entire devotion to you: how much more deeply then must I feel for you knowing you love me."*

March, 1820

Sweetest Fanny,

You fear, sometimes, I do not love you so much as you wish? My dear Girl I love you ever and ever and without reserve. The more I have known you the more have I lov'd. In every way – even my jealousies have been agonies of Love, in the hottest fit I ever had I would have died for you. I have vex'd you too much. But for Love! Can I help it? You are always new. The last of your kisses was ever the sweetest; the last smile the brightest; the last movement the gracefullest. When you pass'd my window home yesterday, I was fill'd with as much admiration as if I had then seen you for the first time. You uttered a half complaint once that I only lov'd your Beauty. Have I nothing else then to love in you but that? Do not I see a heart naturally furnish'd with wings imprison itself with me? No ill prospect has been able to turn your thoughts a moment from me. This perhaps should be as much a subject of sorrow as joy – but I will not talk of that. Even if you did not love me I could not help an entire devotion to you: how much more deeply then must I feel for you knowing you love me. My Mind has been the most discontented and restless one that ever was put into a body too small for it. I never felt my Mind repose upon anything with complete and undistracted enjoyment – upon no person but you. When you are in the room my thoughts never fly out of window: you always concentrate my whole senses. The anxiety shown about our Love in your last note is an immense pleasure to me; however you must not suffer such speculations to molest you any more: not will I any more believe you can have the least pique against me. Brown is gone out — but here is Mrs Wylie — when she is gone I shall be awake for you. — Remembrances to your Mother.

Your affectionate,

J. Keats

But with his health deteriorating fast, at times he (Keats) is envious too!

(?) March 1820: "I envied Sam 's walk with you to day; which I will not do again as I may get very tired of envying."

March (?) 1820

My dearest Girl,

In consequence of our company I suppose I shall not see you before tomorrow. I am much better to day – indeed all I have to complain of is want of strength and a little tightness in the Chest. I envied Sam 's walk with you to day; which I will not do again as I may get very tired of envying. I imagine you now sitting in your new black dress which I like so much and if I were a little less selfish and more enthusiastic I should run round and surprise you with a knock at the door. I fear I am too prudent for a dying kind of Lover. Yet, there is a great difference between going off in warm blood like Romeo, and making one 's exit like a frog in a frost – I had nothing particular to say to day, but not intending that there shall be any interruption to our correspondence (which at some future time I propose offering to Murray) […].

God bless you my sweet Love.

Illness is a long lane, but I see you at the end of it, and shall mend my pace as well as possible

J-K

Failing health makes him bitter and jealous: Keats accuses Fanny of flirtation with his friend Charles Brown

Despite treatment and constant care of his friends, Keats's condition continued to worsen; he became so weak he could barely manage a quarter of an hour in the garden. Fanny was there by his side. The doctors, however, advised to keep their visits to a minimum. Keats was to avoid any heightened emotion, any upset.

Keats's own medical training countered any optimism. He foresaw his death with brutal clarity; so he wrote to Fanny, telling her she was free to break their engagement. She passionately refused. Though it was his own proposal, Keats was relieved: *"How hurt I should have been had you ever acceded to what is, notwithstanding, very reasonable!"*

On 6 March, 1820, Keats had a new and dangerous symptom. That night, he experienced violent palpitations of the heart. A new doctor was called in; he declared Keats to be suffering from a primarily hysterical illness caused by anxiety. Brown was relieved. He wrote to Taylor, their common friend and publisher of Keats's works, that *"there is no pulmonary affection, no organic defect whatever – the disease is on his mind"*. This diagnosis reinforced his earlier impression that was also shared by most of Keats's friends that Fanny's presence in Keats's life was bad for his health. Keats's exquisite sensitivity, his creative expanse – **the qualities** which made him a great poet also made him far too susceptible to the rigors of love. Keats's friends knew this, but did Fanny?

In May 1820, Keats decided to leave for Kentish Town in a bid to check the ravages of tuberculosis. Over the next months, the two continued their emotional correspondence. The disease had apparently intensified both his love and jealousy. And in bitterness, in a letter dated July 5, 1820, Keats wrote to Fanny accusing her of flirting with his closest friend, Charles Brown:[140]

July 5, 1820

"Love is not a plaything"

"Wednesday, Morning

My Dearest Girl,

I have been a walk this morning with a book in my hand, but as usual I have been occupied with nothing but you: I wish I could say in an agreeable manner. I am tormented day and night. They talk of my going to Italy. 'Tis certain I shall never recover if I am to be so long separate from you; yet with all this devotion to you I cannot persuade myself into any confidence of you.

---

[140] Keats, John: *"The complete poetical works and letters of John Keats"*, Cambridge Edition, Boston and New York, Houghton, Mifflin and Company, The University Press, Cambridge, 1899, pp. 438-439.

Past experience connected with the fact of my long separation from you gives me agonies which are scarcely to be talked of. When your mother comes I shall be very sudden and expert in asking her whether you have been to Mrs. Dilke's, for she might say no to make me easy. I am literally worn to death, which seems my only recourse. [...] I cannot forget what has pass'd. What? nothing with a man of the world, but to me dreadful. I will get rid of this as much as possible. When you were in the habit of flirting with Brown you would have let off, could your own heart have felt one half of one pang mine did. Brown is a good sort of man – he did not know he was doing me to death by inches. I feel the effect of every one of those hours in my side now; and for that cause, though he has done me many services, though I know his love and friendship for me, though at this moment I should be without pence were it not for his assistance, I will never see or speak to him until we are both old men, if we are to be. I will resent my heart having been made a foot-ball.' Poor boy!"

How have you pass'd this month? Who have you smil'd with? All this may seem savage in me. You do not feel as we do –you do not know what it is to love --one day you may --- your time is not come.

Ask yourself how many unhappy hours Keats has caused you in Loneliness. For myself I have been a Martyr the whole time, and for this reason I speak; the confession is forc'd from me by the torture. I appeal to you by the blood of that Christ you believe in: Do not write to me if you have done anything this month which it would have pained me to have seen You may have altered – if you have not – if you still behave in dancing rooms and other societies as I have seen you – I do not want to live – if you have done so I wish this coming night may be my last.

I cannot live without you, and not only you but chaste you; virtuous you. The Sun rises and sets, the day passes, and you follow the bent of your inclination to a certain extent – you have no conception of the quantity of miserable feeling that passes through me in a day. Be serious! Love is not a plaything – and again do not write unless you can do it with a crystal conscience. I would sooner die for want of you than ----

Yours for ever

J. KEATS."

Adieu Fanny: Keats prepares to leave for Rome

Beginning early May, Keats had been living at 2 Wesleyan Place, Kentish Town, around the corner from his friend and one-time mentor Leigh Hunt. After a bout of blood-spitting (technically, haemoptysis) on 22 June, the next day by invitation Keats moves in with the Hunts at 13 Mortimer Terrace so that his condition can be monitored. While at the Hunt residence, Keats becomes very upset when he discovers that a letter to him from Fanny is opened (unintentionally, it seems) by someone in the Hunt household, and so he leaves in a distraught state. Not long after, Keats apologizes for his exaggerated response; he lets Hunt know as much, and that he feels genuinely touched by Hunt's patience and many sympathies (letter to Leigh Hunt, 13 Aug).

After about seven weeks staying with Hunt and Hunt's somewhat hectic family (with five children running around) at Mortimer Terrace in Kentish Town, Keats on 12 August returns to Wentworth Place in Hampstead to stay with the Brawne family: a widowed mother with her three children, one to whom Keats is betrothed. named Fanny, and Keats wears her ring. Keats had formerly stayed in the other half of Wentworth Place (a detached double-house, which, in English terms, is called a villa). It has been a wet summer, and poor Keats is not in very good shape, and the sympathies and care of Mrs. Brawne are considerable.

Keats's situation and pronounced nervous state both magnify and twist his regard for Fanny Brawne. Over July and into August, Keats in fatalistic terms tells her that he cannot live without her. He is possessive and jealous in the extreme, and, by throwing out frantic ultimatums, he emotionally manipulates her by attempting to control her behaviour and feelings. I am sickened at the brute world which you are smiling with, he writes to her. I hate men and women more. The world, he says, is too brutal, and he says that only in the grave might he have some rest. Keats's feelings for Fanny have fallen into and merged with other parts of his distressed state and situation, so much so that at moments despondency and anger take command over his emotional life.

With medical advice and the support of others who are very worried about him, Keats since early July seriously considers a move to Italy in an attempt to restore his deteriorating health. Those close to him note his extremely poor and increasingly emaciated state. By mid-August, it is determined that he will go to Italy. Keats writes, *"another winter in England would, I have not a doubt, kill me"*. Therefore, as advised by the doctors, Keats decides to leave for Rome in September.

On 11 September 1820, Fanny wrote Keats's farewell to his sister (also named 'Frances'); and *"with* [Fanny's] *consent he* [Keats]*destroyed the letters she had sent him."* Before leaving, Keats and Fanny exchanged gifts:

> "[…] *he offered her his copy of "The Cenci" and the treasured facsimile of the folio Shakespeare in which he had written his comments and the sonnet on King Lear. He gave her an Etruscan lamp and his miniature, the perfect likeness which his painter friend Severn had painted of him."*

Fanny gave him a new pocket-book, a journal and paper so that he could write to her. She lined his travelling cap with silk, and gave him a lock of her hair, taking one of his own in exchange. In the hope of cooling his encroaching fever, she also gave him a carnelian stone – an oval white marble with which she used to cool her hands while sewing. This marble, which Fanny herself had clasped so often, would rarely leave Keats's hands in Rome.

The journey became more pressing by the end of August. Keats had another severe haemorrhage and was now confined to bed, nursed diligently by Fanny.

To defray the cost of journey to Rome as well as the cost of treatment there, money was needed. Taylor was generous as always, and eager to help Keats. The success of Keats's last volume of poems helped Taylor to advance money for the trip. He also wrote to James Clark, a Scottish doctor, who practised in Rome. Clark was eager to help. He was familiar with Keats's name; he had read his *"Endymion"* and become a great admirer of Keats.

Keats wrote to Brown, his closest friend, who was in Scotland at that time, asking him to accompany to Rome. Brown hurried back to London; but Keats had departed by that time.

But who would accompany him? Brown had not returned. Amongst his other close friends, Hunt, Haslam, and Dilke had families and Haydon was busy. On 12 September, his painter friend, Joseph Severn was approached.

The young painter was an ardent admirer of Keats; he had just won the Academy Gold Medal which provided him a travelling fellowship. A season in Rome could benefit Keats's health and Severn's painting. Severn accepted the charge; though young and inexperienced, he proved to be an admirable friend for the ailing poet in his worst hour of crisis.

Keats needed the sunshine of Rome for recovery; but he dreaded the trip. He did not dare believe he would return. The parting from Fanny, with whom he had become so intimate, would be heart-breaking.

As for Fanny, it was painful too. From their surviving love letters, it transpires she and Keats had fallen even more deeply in love during their last month together. The task of nursing Keats could have destroyed her affection, but, surprisingly, instead it deepened and strengthened her love.[141]

---

[141] Richardson, Joanna. *"Fanny Brawne: A Biography"*, Norwich: Jarrold and Sons, 1952.

Chapter 18
Shelley invites Keats to join him in Italy

"till the Future dares
Forget the Past, his fate and fame shall be
An echo and a light unto eternity!"

["*Adonais*" by Percy Bysshe Shelly]

In the summer of 1818, Keats went on a walking tour in the Lake District of northern England and Scotland with his friend Charles Brown; his exposure and over exertions on that trip brought on him the first symptoms of the tuberculosis of which he was to die. It was aggravated further as he engaged himself with the nursing care for his brother, Tom, who had contracted tuberculosis

In early 1820, Keats began to exhibit symptoms of tuberculosis. His second volume of poems was published in July. Perhaps Keats's greatest (and the only) relief about this time was that his 1820 volume "*Lamia, Isabella, The Eve of St. Agnes, and Other Poems*" (1820) was published between 26 June and 3 July. It receives decent reviews with what Keats, in a letter dated 14 August 1820 to Charles Brown, called the "literary people", and that sale, he wrote in this letter, was moderate. It was generally acknowledged that the volume displayed vast power and genius, and more favourable reviews had begun to appear.

At the end of August, Keats haemorrhages again, and his prospects and strength decline further. He reports a couple of times that his chest is tight and agitated. Everything, it seems, taxes and tires him. In a letter dated 13 August to his sister Frances he writes, "*I am excessively nervous*". His young painter friend Joseph Severn reports that in July Keats's appearance is shocking, and that it reminds him of how Keats's younger brother, Tom, looked before he died of consumption in December 1818.

For quite some time since early July, Keats was seriously considering to move to Italy in an attempt to restore his sinking health. Keats's doctors and well-wishers had all advised him to go to Italy, particularly to Rome, that boasts a surfeit of sunshine and as early as February, is warm enough for sundresses and picnic. Shelley, his friend, was in Pisa at that time. Shelley had left England two years ago, in 1818.

While in England, Shelley came to know Keats, and they were friendly too, but not too close. Shelley, in particular, liked the young poet and his poems although the latter's earlier published work *'Endymion'* had been subject to savage criticism by a section of critics. Shelley was relatively more fortunate. When his *"The Revolt of Islam"* was published, Blackwood's went out of the way to say that *"unlike Keats, Shelley was at least a gentleman."*

Once established at Pisa, Shelley found himself at the peak of his poetic power. Here he wrote *"Ode to the West Wind"*, *"To a Skylark"*, and other great poems. The universe, in the phrase of Francis Thompson, became a *'box of toys for the enchanted child,"* and *"he danced in and out of the gates of Heaven: its floor was littered with his broken fancies [...]"*.[142]

About this time Shelley received the information that a new volume of poems by Keats (*"Lamia, Isabella, The Eve of St. Agnes and Other poems"*) had just appeared in London, and for the first time was enjoying a good critical reception. But with this came the reports of his illness and failing health, Shelley promptly invited Keats to join him in Italy. In a letter dated 27 July 1820, full of warmth as well as appreciation for Keats's genius, he wrote:

"... you are capable of the greatest things ..."

"Pisa, 27th July, 1820

My Dear Keats,

I hear with great pain the dangerous accident you have undergone, and Mrs. Gisborne, who gives me the account of it, adds that you continue to wear a consumptive appearance. This consumption is particularly fond of people who write such good verses as you have done, and with the assistance of an English winter it can often

---

[142] Schuster, M. Lincoln: *"The World's Great Letters"*, Simon & Schuster Inc. New York City, New York, 1940, p.237-239.

indulge its selection. I do not think that young and amiable poets are bound to gratify its taste; they have entered into no bond with the Muses to that effect.

But seriously (for I am joking on what I am very serious about) I think you would do well to pass the winter after so tremendous an accident in Italy, and if you think it as necessary as I do, so long as you continue to find Pisa or its neighbourhood agreeable to you, Mrs. Shelley unites with myself in urging the request, that you would take up with us. You might come by sea to Leghorn (France is not worth seeing and the sea is particularly good for weak lungs), which is within a few miles of us. You ought, at all events, to see Italy, and your health which I suggest as a motive, might be an excuse to you.

Percy Bysshe Shelley

I spare declamation about the statues, and the paintings, and the ruins, and what is a greater piece of forbearance, about the mountains streams and fields, the colours of the sky, and the sky itself.

I have lately read your "Endymion" again and even with a new sense of the treasures of poetry it contains, though treasures poured forth with indistinct profusion. This, people in general, will not endure, and that is the cause of the comparatively few copies which have been sold. I feel persuaded that you are capable of the greatest things, so you but will.

I always tell Ollier to send you copies of my books. – "Prometheus Unbound" I imagine you will receive nearly at the same time with this letter. "The Cenci" I hope you have already received – it was studiously composed in a different style.

"Below the good how far! But far above the great."

In poetry I have sought to avoid system and mannerism; I wish those who excel me in genius would pursue the same plan.

Whether you remain in England, or journey to Italy, believe that you carry with you my anxious wishes for your health, happiness and success, wherever you are, or whatever you undertake, and that I am,

Yours sincerely,

P.B. Shelley."

John Keats acknowledges the invitation to visit Shelley at Pisa

About three weeks letter, on the 16 August 1820, Keats replies quite appreciatively accepting Shelley's invitation: He also offers some gentle criticism of Shelley's poetic style and output and observes, that he [Shelley] *"would better curb his magnanimity, and be more of an artist, and load every rift of* [his] *subject with ore.* Keats in his letter remembers Shelley once advised him not to publish immature or early poetry—"*first blights*", Keats calls them, referring to the overall quality of his own early work. Keats also comments to Shelley that he wishes he could "*unwrite*" his immature long poem, 'Endymion'.

"My imagination is a monastery, and I am its monk ...."

"Hampstead, August, 1820

My Dear Shelley,

I am very much gratified that you, in a foreign country, and with a mind almost over-occupied, should write to me in the strain of the letter beside me. If I do not take advantage of your invitation, it will be prevented by a circumstance I have very much to heart to prophesy. There is no doubt that an English winter would put an end to me, and do so in a lingering, hateful manner. Therefore, I must either voyage or journey to Italy, as a soldier marches up to a battery.

My nerves at present are the worst part of me, yet they feel soothed that, come what extreme may, I shall not be destined to remain in one spot long enough to take a hatred of any four particular bedposts. I am glad you take any pleasure in my poor poem, which I would willingly take the trouble to unwrite, if possible, did I care so much as I have done about reputation. I received a copy of "The Cenci" as from yourself, from Hunt. There is only one part of it I am judge of — the poetry and dramatic effect, which by many spirits now a days is considered the Mammon.

A modern work, it is said, must have a purpose, which may be the God. An artist must serve Mammon; he must have "self-concentration" — selfishness, perhaps. You, I am sure, will forgive me for sincerely remarking that you might curb your magnanimity, and be more of an artist, and load every rift of your subject with ore. The thought of such discipline must fall like cold chains upon you, who perhaps never sat with your wings furled for six months together.

And is not this extraordinary talk for the writer of "Endymion", whose mind was like a pack of scattered cards? I am picked up and sorted to a pip.

My imagination is a monastery, and I am its monk. I am in expectation of "Prometheus" every day. Could I have my own wish effected, you would have it still in manuscript, or be now putting an end to the second act. I remember you advising me not to publish my first blights, on Hampstead Heath. I am returning advice upon your hands. Most of the poems in the volume I send you, have been written over two years, and would never have been published but for hope of gain; so you see I am inclined enough to take your advice now. I must express once more my deep sense of your kindness, adding my sincere thanks and respects for Mrs. Shelley.

In the hope of soon seeing you,

I remain most sincerely yours,

John Keats"[143]

The following month, on 13 September, 1820, Keats set out for Italy with his artist friend Severn, who was planning to study art in Rome. On arrival in

---

[143] Ibid., 240-241.

Italy, they moved into a two-room apartment in a villa on the Spanish Steps in Rome.

But his hope of seeing Shelley soon, as he had desired in his reply to the latter's invitation, remained unfulfilled. Shortly after he reached Rome, Keats grew progressively worse, and a trip to Pisa was out of question. The two never met again.

Chapter 19
On board the 'Maria Crowther': Keats sails for Italy

For going to Italy, Keats needed to somehow raise money as well as find someone to accompany him. He hoped he would go with his very good friend Charles Brown, with whom he has previously lived and travelled. By the end of the month, Keats asked for money from his family guardian Richard Abbey; Abbey refused to give him anything, claiming his own financial difficulties. Keats barely managed to get by with loans from generous friends like John Taylor and Brown. Keats apparently spent up his own means, having lived for a couple of years based on credit from that share, inherited from his maternal grandmother. He was, however, unaware that a considerable sum (perhaps about 800 pounds) was actually available to him via the courts (Chancery), left to him by his maternal grandfather (in today's terms, perhaps approximately, £80,000). It appears Abbey was also unaware of this money, which had been growing with interest.

His Last Will

Keats was definitely anxious as to what would happen to him having seen his own mother and younger brother, Tom die from consumption. Yet, on 13 August, 1820 he said he half believed his illness was not yet Consumption, and ten days later he expressed some hopes of "cheating the consumption". However, during mid-August, perhaps knowing he will die quite soon, he composed a short will wherein he writes to his publisher, the loyal and generous John Taylor: "*In case of my death this scrap of paper may be serviceable in your possession.*" The will stipulates that his friend Brown and John Taylor be first paid from his estate, and that his books be divided among his friends.[144]

---

[144] "*12 August, 1820: Keats: "Excessively Nervous" & "Cheating the Consumption*", Mapping Keats's Progress: A Critical Chronology. https://shorturl.at/jmnvN

> **Keats's Last Will**
>
> *"All my estate real and personal consists in the hopes of the sale of books publish'd or unpublish'd. Now I wish Brown and you to be the first paid Creditors — the rest is in nubibus [in the clouds], but in case it should shower pay my Taylor the few pounds I owe him.*
>
> *"My chest of books I divide among my friends."*
>
> --- John Keats

September 17, 1820: Keats on board the sailing brig 'Maria Crowther'

Having thus prepared for eventualities back at home in the event of the worst happening in the days ahead, Keats decided to leave for Italy without further delay to catch some sunshine in Rome lest the ensuing winter further acts upon his health. So, on 13 September, 1820 he, accompanied by his painter friend Severn, left for Gravesend and four days later they boarded '*Maria Crowther*', a single decked 130 ton two-masted brig built in 1810. Four passengers and the captain[145] all shared the one cabin. The voyage was long, lasting 38 days and was beset by storms. Keats's friends, Taylor, Haslam, and Woodhouse accompanied him to Gravesend, and left him on 17 September at 4 o'clock in the afternoon.

Severn initially had no clear idea regarding the seriousness of Keats's illness. It was only a week or so into the voyage that Severn began to realise the gravity of the problem. Keats grew feverish during the night, coughed hard and brought up blood. But the most disturbing to Severn was the mental agony that Keats was passing through. He often stood all alone on the deck, staring silently over the dark water. As Severn wrote, *"He was often so distraught, with moreover so sad a look in his eyes, sometimes a starved, haunting expression that it bewildered me."*

---

[145] Keats, Severn, Miss Cotterell, Mrs Pidgeon and The Master, Thomas Walsh.

'*Maria Crowther*', Sailing brig painted by Joseph Severn

During the voyage, Severn found Keats withdrawn and difficult to reach. The silence unnerved him; he gradually became aware of **another reason for** Keats's agony – it wasn't simply his ill health; it was also an ill-fated love affair he had with a young girl in London named Fanny Brawne. Severn knew of Fanny, but he did not know that she and Keats were engaged. Their engagement – **both Keats and Fanny had tried their best to keep a secret.** Throughout the voyage, Keats would think only of Fanny, she was the focus of his conversation with Severn.

Joseph Severn
(from a drawing by his daughter Mary, 1849)

During the voyage, despite his failing health and mental agony, Keats made the final revision of his poem "*Bright Star*".

Chapter 20
Keats's Last Sonnet: "Bright Star"

> ### *Bright Star*
>
> *"Bright star, would I were stedfast as thou art—*
> *Not in lone splendour hung aloft the night*
> *And watching, with eternal lids apart,*
> *Like nature's patient, sleepless Eremite,*
> *The moving waters at their priestlike task*
> *Of pure ablution round earth's human shores,*
> *Or gazing on the new soft-fallen mask*
> *Of snow upon the mountains and the moors—*
> *No—yet still stedfast, still unchangeable,*
> *Pillow'd upon my fair love's ripening breast,*
> *To feel for ever its soft fall and swell,*
> *Awake forever in a sweet unrest,*
> *Still, still to hear her tender-taken breath,*
> *And so live ever—or else swoon to death."*
>
> [John Keats, "*Bright Star*"]

While on his voyage to Italy for treatment, Keats wrote his last sonnet *"Bright Star"*, The poem came to be forever associated with the "*Bright Star*" of his life, Fanny Brawne -- his yearning and inspiration. It was a "*declaration of his* [Keats's] *love*" to her.

Keats had initially drafted this poem sometime earlier and perfected it later in 1820 while he was travelling to Rome for treatment. It is, however, not quite clear when he first drafted "*Bright Star*"; his biographers suggest different dates.

Keats remained reticent and did not talk about the "*Bright Star*" sonnet or about his relationship with Fanny even to his most intimate friends except

Charles Brown. Keats's reticence has led some scholars to raise questions on this subject. Commenting upon Keats's reticence, Naomi J. Kirk remarks,[146]

> *"There was not any shame in his reticence; his love was a holy of holies in which he did not invite his closest friends, much less wish to have it invaded by the vulgarly curious."*

In 1846, twenty-five years after Keats's death, a letter by his friend, Severn, concerning the composition of the *"Bright Star"* sonnet was published in the *'Union Magazine'*:

"*21, James Street*

Jan. 21st, 1846

Sir,

Through the medium of the Union Magazine, I have the gratification to present the public with an unpublished MS. Poem of Keats', (the last he ever wrote,) which I trust may be admired and well received, as the harbinger of many other unpublished works of the illustrious young poet, now editing [sic] by Mr. R. Monckton Milnes.

The present exquisite Sonnet was written under such interesting circumstances that I cannot forbear making them public. Keats and myself were beating about the British Channel in the autumn of 1820, anxiously waiting for a wind to take us to Italy, which place, together with the sea-voyage were deemed likely to preserve his life; for he was then in a state of consumption, which left but the single hope of an Italian sojourn to save him. The stormy British sea, after a fortnight, had exhausted him; and on our arrival at off the Dorsetshire coast, having at last the charm of a fine and tranquil day, we landed to recruit.

The shores, with the beautiful grottoes which opened to fine verdure and cottages, were the means of transporting Keats once more into the region of poetry; -- he showed these things exultingly, as though they had been his birth right. The change in him was wonderful; and continued even after our return to the ship, when we took a volume

---

[146] Kirk, Naomi J.: *"The Girl who shared Keats's Fate*: "In Praise of Lady Dead and—'"*, American Scholar, 6 (1937), p. 49.

(which he had a few days before given me) of Shakespeare's Poems and in it he wrote the subjoined Sonnet, which at the time I thought the most enchanting of all his efforts. Twenty-five years have passed away, and I have by degrees (in the love I bear to his memory) placed it in my mind as among the most enchanting poetry of the world.

After writing this Sonnet, Keats sank down into a melancholy state, and never wrote again, save one painful letter on the same subject as the Sonnet – for the love so rapturously sung in it was then hastening the poet's death: it was a real and honourable love, which, but for the separation occasioned by his direful illness, would have been blessed in a happy and advantageous marriage. Alas! For Italy --- he only went there to die.

I remain, Sir,

Yours truly,

Joseph Severn."

In 1848, the noted English poet and patron of literature, Richard Monckton Milnes, 1st Baron Houghton, included the sonnet *"Bright Star"* in his seminal work *"Life, Letters, and Literary Remains of John Keats"*.[147] When he printed the poem from the copy Keats had made for Severn on board the *'Maria Crowther'*, he repeated Severn's account of the poem which implied Keats had composed it that very day, his last on English soil. Severn believed that it was Keats's last ever poem and that it had been composed especially for him. Based on Milnes's work, September 28, 1820 came to be widely accepted as the date of composition of the sonnet *"Bright Star"*.

The position, however, changed when Sir Sidney Colvin, the noted English literary and art critic, brought to the fore an earlier version of *"Bright Star"* transcribed by Charles Brown and dated 1819.[148] This transcript, however, offered no clue to a precise date in 1819; and thereafter, the sonnet has been assigned to all four seasons of that year.

---

[147] Milnes, Richard Monckton (ed.): *"The Life, Letters, and Literary Remains of John Keats"*, London, Edward Moxon, Dover Street, 1848.

[148] Colvin, Sidney. *"John Keats: His Life and Poetry, His Friends, Critics and After-Fame"*, London: Macmillan, 1917.

M.B. Forman, who edited *"The Letters of John Keats"*, notes that the poem *"Bright star"* had been published twice before 1848, the 1820 version by Severn in 1846, the 1819 version by Brown in 1838, and that Milnes must have been familiar with the earlier version as well in published or perhaps, even in transcript form, for Brown had entrusted him to put together the *"Life, Letters, and Literary Remains"* of Keats's works and for doing so, he loaned him all his manuscripts for use. Forman, therefore, wryly remarks, *"Milnes's motives ... for following Severn's story and ignoring Brown's date are puzzling, to say the least"*.

Colvin believed Keats composed *"Bright Star"* in the last week of February 1819, *"probably before dawn on the actually morning of the 25th"*, immediately after his informal engagement with Fanny. Ernest de Selincourt, the English literary scholar and critic, tentatively accepted Colvin's date in his edition, but he also suggested two alternatives, namely, July and the late autumn of 1819.[149]

Aileen Ward, the American professor of English literature who won both a National Book Award and a Duff Cooper Memorial Prize for her book *"John Keats: The Making of a Poet"*, has, however, challenged Colvin's proposition, particularly because it is by now well established that Keats became engaged to Fanny in October, 1819 and not in February 1819, as Colvin supposed.[150]

Keats's biographer, Amy Lowell assigns the sonnet to April, 1819 pointing out that in one of his *"Scotch letters"* to his brother Tom, written on 25 June, 1818, Keats had described his first sight of Windermere as refining his *"sensual vision into a sort of north star which can never cease to be open-lidded and stedfast over the wonders of the great Power"* – a metaphor strikingly similar to the image of the star *"watching with eternal lids apart"* in the sonnet. Lowell notes the parallel and then indicates a missing link between the passages in a letter of the following spring that Keats wrote on April 15, 1819 to his brother George and sister-in-law Georgiana in America; in that letter, he mentioned that he had found some *"letters to from you and poor Tom and me"* at his old lodgings. Assuming that the Scotch journal was

---

[149] Selincourt, Ernest de: *"The Poems of John Keats"*, London, 1951, p. 576.
[150] Ward, Aileen: *"The Date of Keats's "Bright Star" Sonnet"*, Studies in Philology, Vol. 52, No. 1 (Jan., 1955), University of North Carolina Press, p. 75-85.

there in the lot, Lowell suggests that when Keats reread it the image of the north star "*stuck in his head and became incorporated in* [the] *sonnet* [which] *he wrote very soon after*" --- probably on the 15th, 16th or the 17th of April. In support of her thesis, she, inter alia, cites the fact that moon was waning that week; Keats may, therefore, have been struck by the unusual brilliance of the stars in the early part of the night. Finally, she points out, the sonnet clearly expresses Keats's prevailing mood that spring – "*doubt, doubt, always doubt of Fanny Brawne's constancy*".[151]

Ward dismisses Lowell's proposition, on several counts, particularly on the ground that the feelings expressed in the sonnet do not fit well with what is known of Keats's thoughts and moods in the middle of April. 1819. He had many small worries on his mind at the time, but his spirits were high and rose still higher as the spring wore on. "*There is no hint of any desire for annihilation in love such as the sonnet expresses, or of the gnawing doubts about Fanny which Lowell – on the strength of this poem alone – attributed to him. Rather, from all we know, the Brawnes' moving into Wentworth Place that April ushered in the happiest month of Keats's life.*"

'Bright Star': Who's the Star? Fanny Brawne or Isabella Jones?

Biographer Andrew Motion, Poet Laureate of the United Kingdom from 1999 to 2009, suggests the sonnet was begun in October 1819. Gittings, on the contrary, is of the view the first version of "*Bright Star*" was written not in 1819 but in April, 1818 before he met his beloved Fanny Brawne –and, in an interesting twist to the whole issue, he also suggests that it was addressed not to Fanny Brawne but to Isabella Jones, with whom Keats had an affair before he met Fanny.

Ward questions Gittings's conclusion; she points out that Brown's transcript is clearly dated 1819. Gittings sought to defend his stand arguing that it "*only shows the year in which Brown copied it*". Ward disagrees and shows that after starting his book of transcripts in the spring of 1819, Brown copied at least fourteen of Keats's transcripts, assigning ten of them to 1817 or 1818 and leaving four uncertain ones undated; each of his dates, therefore, clearly referred to the year of composition. Furthermore, Ward argues, Gittings quoted a number of undoubted parallels between the letters and the

---

[151] Lowell, Amy: "*John Keats*", Boston, Houghton Mifflin Company, 1925.

poems which Keats is known to have written or read in October, 1818, but the parallels he drew between these and the *"Bright Star"* or sonnet are not convincing.

So October, 1818 seems as unlikely as most other suggestions for the date of *"Bright Star"*; but, what about July or the autumn of 1819, as suggested by Selincourt, as a possible date. Interestingly, **Dorothy Hewlett** and **Joanna Richardson** also advocated for 25 July, 1819 as the date of the '*Bright Star*' sonnet?

In her article titled *"The Date of Keats's "Bright Star" Sonnet"*, published in 1955, Ward examines all these suggestions in great detail and concludes that July, 1819 is perhaps the most probable date when the sonnet was first drafted. The last word on the subject is, however, yet to be said and the issue is open for further research.

Keats, as stated earlier, perfected the final version of the sonnet on 28 September, 1820 on board the brig *"Maria Crowther"*, while on his way to Rome. It was copied into a volume of *"The Poetical Works of William Shakespeare"*, opposite Shakespeare's poem, '*A Lover's Complaint*'. The book had been given to Keats in 1819 by his close friend and poet, John Hamilton Reynolds.

The *"Bright Star"* was officially published in 1838 in *The Plymouth and Devonport Weekly Journal*, 17 years after Keats's death.[152][153]

---

[152] Gittings, Robert: *"John Keats"* Heinemann, 1968.
[153] Sugano, Michio: *"Was 'Keats's Last Sonnet' Really Written on Board the Maria Crowther?"*, Studies in Romanticism, Vol. 34, No. 3, On Keats in 1995 (Fall, 1995), pp. 413-440.

Chapter 21
Keats arrives at Naples

"Is there another Life? Shall I awake and find all this a dream? There must be we cannot be created for this sort of suffering."

-- John Keats

October 21, 1820: At Naples

On 21 October 1820, Keats arrived at Naples harbour. Unfortunately for Keats, the sea voyage was not at all smooth. There were misfortunes galore on the way; storms broke out followed by a dead calm that slowed the ship's progress. Even when they finally reached Naples, the ship was held in the city's harbour for 10 days (not nearly the '*quaranta giorni*' — 40 days — that give us the word quarantine) for the cholera pandemic, which lasted from 1817-1824, had spread to London at the time. Moreover, Naples was also then dealing with a typhus outbreak; so they did not want another disease to ransack them, and forced the vessel Keats was on to quarantine.[154]

The unpleasantness of being stuck for ten days on a single-masted brig like 'Maria Crowther' was especially intense because the extra days were tacked onto a wretched voyage. "The passage out of the Thames into the Channel was predictably rough," Andrew Motion[155] writes, with "cross-currents churn[ing] the water into angry waves". As the ship sailed past Brighton, gale-storm winds kicked up, and waves washed across the ship. Even before the weather turned rough, the travellers were queasy. Keats's companion Joseph Severn vomited over the side of the boat; a consumptive fellow passenger, Miss Cotterell, fainted.

---

[154] "*John Keats and His Ten Day Quarantine*", Cove. https://shorturl.at/gmxBI

[155] Motion, Andrew: "*Keats*", London: Faber, 1997.

During the period of quarantine, despite his ill health, Keats invented puns; he read Byron.. He also set down the events of his life in order to make sense of it. The document is a painful read.

The strain and fatigue of the long and arduous journey acted upon his health. The long separation and absence of communication from his love added further to his agony. As his condition deteriorated, Keats became more and more restless. On 1 November, 1820, immediately after being let out of quarantine at Naples, he wrote to his friend Charles Armitage Brown of his desperation and love for Fanny:[156]

November 1, 1820, Keats's letter to Charles Brown: "Was I born for this end?"

"Naples, November 1 [1820]

MY DEAR BROWN,

Yesterday we were let out of quarantine, during which my health suffered more from bad air and the stifled cabin that it had done the whole voyage. The fresh air revived me a little, and I hope I am well enough this morning to write to you a short calm letter; -- if that can be called one, in which I am afraid to speak of what I would fainest dwell upon. As I have gone thus far into it, I must go on a little; -- perhaps it may relieve the load of WRETCHEDNESS which possess upon me. The persuasion that I shall see her no more will kill me. My dear Brown, I should have had her when I was in health, and I should have remained well. I can bear to die – I cannot bear to leave her. Oh, God! God! God! Everything I have in my trunks that reminds me of her goes through me like a spear. The silk lining she put in my travelling cap scalds my head. My imagination is horridly vivid about her – I see her – I hear her. There is nothing in the world of sufficient interest to divert me from her for a moment. This was the case when I was in England; I cannot recollect, without shuddering, the time that I was a prisoner at Hunt's, and used to keep my eyes fixed at Hampstead all day. Then there was a good hope of seeing her again ---Now! – O that I could be buried near where she lives! 'I am afraid to write to her – to receive a letter from her – to see her hand-

---

[156] Keats, John: "*The complete poetical works and letters of John Keats*", Cambridge Edition, Boston and New York, Houghton, Mifflin and Company, The University Press, Cambridge, 1899, pp. 447-448.

writing would break my heart – even to hear of her anyhow, to see her name written, would be more than I could bear–' My dear Brown, what am I to do? Where can I look for consolation or ease? If I had any chance of recovery, this passion would kill me. Indeed through the whole of my illness, both at your house and at Kentish Town, this fever has never ceased wearing me out. When you write to me, which you will do immediately, write to Rome (poste restante) --- if she is well and happy, put a mark thus +; if --.

Remember me to all. I will endeavour to bear my miseries patiently. A person in my state of health should not have such miseries to bear. Write a short note to my sister, saying you have heard from me. Severn is very well. If I were in better heath I would urge your coming to Rome. I fear there is no one who can give me any comfort. Is there any news of George? O that something fortunate had ever happened to me or my brothers! – then I might hope, -- but despair is force upon me as a habit. My dear Brown, for my sake be her advocate for ever. I cannot say a word about Naples; I do not feel at all concerned in the thousand novelties around me. I am afraid to write to her – I should like her to know that I do not forget her. Oh, Brown, I have coals of fire in my breast. It surprises me that the human heart is capable of containing and bearing so much misery. Was I born for this end? God bless her, and her mother, and my sister, and George, and his wife, and you, and all!

Your ever affectionate friend

JOHN KEATS."

As he spent more time with Keats, Severn was convinced the poet's problems were caused as much by love as his physical ailment. This belief gave Severn some optimism since mental agony as such was not as alarming as consumption. But he was disturbed by the intensity of Keats's feeling and its adverse impact upon his health.

Chapter 22
The Death of Adonais

"Land and sea, weakness and decline are great separators, but death is the great divorcer for ever."

-- John Keats

November 14, 1820: In Rome

Keats reached Rome on 14 November, 1820. It was too late by then; the winter was about to set in and there was hardly any hope of the Italian sunshine that he was looking for. By the time he arrived in Rome, he was terminally ill. As the English poet Francis Thompson rightly put it, *"He was first half chewed in London and finally spit dying into Italy."*

On arrival in Italy, he moved into a villa on the Spanish Steps in Rome. Despite care from Severn and Dr. James Clark, his health rapidly deteriorated.

There were times when Keats was hallucinating for lack of oxygen and lack of sustenance.

The treatment advised by Clark did not result in any improvement. Keats's health continued to deteriorate. There seemed to be no hope of recovery and his doctor Clark admitted as much to Keats. The poet's thoughts turned to suicide, driven by his own suffering and memories of his brother Tom's lingering end. Keats begged Severn and Clark for laudanum to mitigate his pain, but both of them refused. Keats grew angry; Severn was keeping him alive against his will. In desperation, he turned to Clark "*how long is this posthumous existence of mine to go on*?" he asked plaintively.

November 30, 1820,

His Last letter: "... I am leading a posthumous existence."

"Rome, November 30, 1820

On 30 November 1820, Keats wrote his last letter, laced with despair, to his friend Brown:[157]

> MY DEAR BROWN,
>
> "Tis the most difficult thing in the world to me to write a letter. My stomach continues so bad that I feel it worse on opening any book – yet I am much better than I was in Quarantine. Then I am afraid to encounter the pro-ing and conn-ing of anything interesting to me in England. I have an [sic] habitual feeling of my real life having past, and that I am leading a posthumous existence [...]"
>
> God bless you!
>
> JOHN KEATS."

On receiving the last letter from Keats, Brown read it out to Brawnes, "*skipping & adding, without the slightest suspicion on their part,*" telling Fanny that "*... Severn expected an early recovery*"; this illusion was sustained, and all of the worst news was kept from Fanny.

On 10 December, Severn returned from an early walk and woke him up. Immediately, Keats began to cough and then vomit blood. Clark was summoned and he promptly bled him. After Clark had departed, Keats left his bed to stumble around the room, telling Severn, "*This day shall be my last.*" Severn feared he would commit suicide and immediately hid all the sharp objects he could find as well as the laudanum Clark had prescribed. Keats remained delirious for the rest of the day; **later he had another violent haemorrhage and bleeding that weakened him into calm.** Over the next few days, he suffered five severe haemorrhages and was regularly bled by Clark, who constantly visited him and put him on a strict diet. Keats begged for food, saying they were starving him.

---

[157] Keats, John: "*The complete poetical works and letters of John Keats*", Cambridge Edition, Boston and New York, Houghton, Mifflin and Company, The University Press, Cambridge, 1899, pp. 448-449.

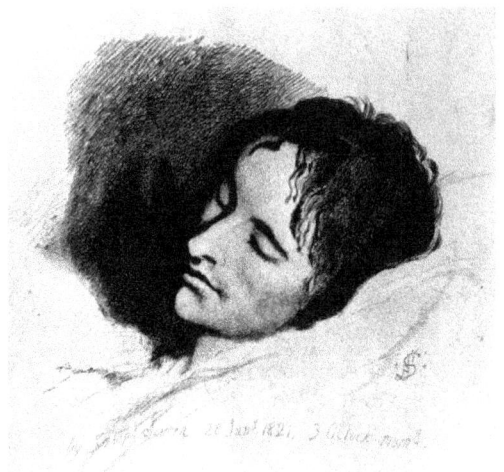

John Keats on his deathbed with tuberculosis aged 25, sedated with laudanum and opium: Painting by Joseph Severn, dated January 28, 1821

As the hope of his recovery receded, his thoughts turned to suicide once more, driven by his own suffering and memories of his brother, Tom's lingering end. As one who had studied medicine, he knew his end was near. *"Keats see all this – his knowledge of anatomy makes it tenfold worse at every change – every way he is unfortunate"*. Clark wrote.

Severn tried to comfort him, but Keats was now past comfort. He rambled on about Tom's illness and death and – what was even more troubling to the devout Severn; he denied any Christian comfort. Severn wrote about it to their friends in England:

> *"For he says in words that tear my very heartstrings – "miserable wretch I am – this last cheap comfort which every rogue and fool have – is deny'd me in my last moments – why is this – O! I have serv'd every one with my utmost good – yet why is this – I cannot understand this"* – and then his chattering teeth *"...I think a malignant being must have power over us – over whom the Almighty has little or no influence – yet you know Severn I cannot believe in your book – the Bible. ...Here am I, with desperation in death that would disgrace the commonest fellow."*

When Severn finished a letter to their friend and Keats's publisher Taylor, the poet told him to add a postscript: *"I shall soon be in a second edition – in sheets – and cold press."*

Severn was a devout Christian. Keats, on the other hand, viewed life as *"a vale of soul-making"*; he was unconcerned with religion. He was a critic of religion who eschewed religious ritual before his death. His famous poem composed in 1816, *"Written in Disgust of Vulgar Superstition"* portrays Christianity as *"dying like an outburnt lamp"*. Even in early 1821 when he was terminally ill, he would still reject Severn's belief in afterlife, and remained committed to his philosophy of 'soul-making' until the end. Severn wrote in mid-January: *"this noble fellow lying on the bed—is dying in horror—no kind hope smoothing down his suffering—no philosophy—no religion to support him."*

His last wish

Keats refused to pray himself; Severn prayed beside him. During his last days, as he lay in bed, his calm was once broken by a letter from his friend Brown, from which fell a note in Fanny's handwriting; the sight shook his nerves. He did not read it, but asked Severn to place it in his coffin, along with a purse made by his sister and a lock of Fanny's hair she gave him before he sailed for Rome.[158]

In January, 1821, his condition deteriorated further; there was a slow and steady decline into the final stage of tuberculosis. Keats coughed hard and was constantly wracked in sweat; his teeth chattered uncontrollably. Severn nursed him devotedly; he observed in a letter how Keats would sometimes cry upon waking to find that he was still alive. On 28 January, Severn sketched Keats as he slept.

Towards the end, his thoughts turned to his final resting-place, the Protestant Cemetery beside the Pyramid of Cestius in Rome. He asked Severn to visit and describe the place for him. Severn told him *"of the daisies and violets which grew there; and of the flocks of goats and sheep which roamed over the graves."* Keats was pleased and desired to be buried there after his demise.[159]

As he lay in his corner room next to the Spanish Steps listening night after night to the constant play of water in the fountain outside, the words from a play of Beaumont and Fletcher ('*Philaster*') kept coming back to him:

---

[158] Richardson, Joanna. *"Fanny Brawne: A Biography"*, Norwich: Jarrold and Sons, 1952.
[159] Bate, Walter Jackson, *"John Keats"*, Harvard, 1964, p. 694.

"As you are living; all your better deeds

Shall be in water writ, but this in marble;"

A week or two before he died, he told Severn he wanted no name upon his grave, no epitaph, but only the words, *"Here lies one whose name was writ in water."*

His last words

On 17 February Taylor received a letter from Severn detailing Keats's suffering. The letter mentioned the doctor was of the opinion Keats should never have left England, for the journey had shortened his life and increased his pain. Keats was in tears. Severn tried to comfort him with thoughts of spring. It was the season Keats loved most, and he would not know it again. Bitterly he wept; while he *"kept continually in his hand* [the] *polished, oval, white carnelian, the gift of his widowing love* [Fanny]*, and at times it seemed his only consolation, the only thing left for him in this world clearly tangible."*

With every passing day, his suffering and agony increased. Severn was in tears. But, to his surprise, Keats was more worried about the effect his illness and death would have on him [Severn] and tried to cheer him as best he could. *"I could perceive in many ways that he was always painfully alive to my situation"*, Severn recalled later. As he rushed about caring for Keats, the poet reassured him: *"Now you must be firm for it will not last long"*.

And then – suddenly and surprisingly – he wanted his books nearby. Severn did not understand why *"this great desire for books came across his mind"*; but got him all the books on hand. Keats was no longer able to read but the very presence of the books, Severn wrote, acted as a *'charm'* and it pleased him beyond measure.

It seemed he would die on Wednesday, 21 February; a new fit of coughing began and he asked Severn to hold him up so he could breathe. But he lingered on for another day.

On Friday the 23 February, at about four in the afternoon, Severn was roused by Keats's call:

"Severn – I – lift me up – I am dying – I shall die easy – don't be frightened – be firm, and thank God it has come."

But it did not come for another seven hours, as he rested in Severn's arms, holding his hand.

> "*I lifted him up in my arms.*" Severn writes "*The phlegm seem'd boiling in his throat, and increased until eleven…*" His breathing was deep and difficult, but he seemed beyond pain. Only once did he speak again, whispering, "*Don't breathe on me – it comes like Ice.*"

Finally, a little before midnight, Keats breathed his last. **The** carnelian, the oval white marble **Fanny had given him, was lying by his side when he died.**

Chapter 23
Doctor's blunders to blame for Keats's agonising death?: A Controversy

"To silence gossip, don't repeat it."

-- John Keats

Keats died of "tuberculosis", known as 'consumption' at that time. It was their family disease that was the cause of death of his mother, younger brother Tom whom he had been living with and nursed till his last days, and also claimed the lives of two of his brother George's children. He may also have had additional exposure to tuberculosis while he was a medical student.

In respect of tuberculosis, the epidemiological condition of that era is summarized below:[160]

> "The maximum morbidity from tuberculosis in England apparently occurred about 1780, when the recorded mortality rate for "consumption" was 1120 per 100,000 population. The peak was coincidental with the early development of what in later years was designated the "industrial revolution" ... The first effect has always been a rise, soon followed by a fall in the tuberculosis rate In London the figure dropped to 716 in the decade 1801-1810 ..."

In contrast, he death rate from tuberculosis of the respiratory system in England and Wales in 1971 was 1.9 per 100,000.[161]

---

[160] Jarcho, Saul: *"Amy Lowell and the Death of John Keats"*, Clio Medica, Vol. 12, No.1, pp. 91-95, 1977.

[161] Consumption in that period was a common disorder. John Marshall (1783–1841) in his book '*Statistics &. Mortality of the Metropolis*' reported that in 1821 one third of all deaths in London were due to consumption and that the total number of deaths from consumption was increasing.. Consumption was known to be a chronic disease that affected all parts of the body. It was recognized from post-mortem studies that tubercles could be found both in the lungs and in the abdominal organs.

In February 1820, after intermittent symptoms that had started about two years previously, Keats, aged twenty-four then, spit out blood. After initial treatment, as his condition worsened, he was advised to leave England for a warmer climate elsewhere. Accordingly, Keats, accompanied by his painter friend Severn, left for Rome to catch some sunshine and for treatment under the Scottish physician Dr. James Clark.[162]

But all in vain. Keats died an agonising death, far away from his home, in Rome, on 23 February, 1821.

Death of John Keats: Controversy

There is, however, a major controversy concerning his doctor, Dr Clark, regarding his management of Keats's terminal illness. Lord (Dr.) Russell Claude Brock (1903-1980), a leading British chest and heart surgeon and one of the pioneers of modern open-heart surgery. In his 1971 Sydenham Lecture, delivered before the Faculty of the History of Medicine of the Society of Apothecaries, criticized Clark's treatment of Keats, concluding that even by 1820 standards, Clark made a very poor evaluation of Keats's fatal illness. He wrote it *"was difficult to condone such a rubbishy assessment."*[163]

In his biography of Keats, Andrew Motion argued that *"Keats's doctors in fact had no reasonable grounds for doubting what was the matter with him. They kept him in the dark either because they were colluding with his deception, or because they were incompetent."*[164]

Walter Wells, in '*A Doctor's Life of John Keats*', questions:

> *"Is it not incredible that this estimable doctor, possessed, like his predecessors, of a reputation for special skill in the knowledge and treatment of diseases of the lungs, should not have recognised at the*

---

[162] Dr. James Clark later became renowned for the treatment of tuberculosis. On 11 November 1837, six months after her accession to the throne, Queen Victoria employed him as her Physician-in-Ordinary; he was also created baronet of St George's Hanover Square, London

[163] Brock, R. C.: "*John Keats and Joseph Severn: The Tragedy of the Last Illness*", London: Keats-Shelley Memorial Association, 1973, p.18.

[164] Motion, Andrew, "*Keats*", London: Faber and Faber, 1997, p.499.

first visit that his patient was undoubtedly a far-advanced subject of pulmonary consumption?"[165]

This argument is developed further by Hillas Smith in his book "*Keats and Medicine*" when he writes:

"In a patient with advanced tuberculosis who has abdominal pain and vomiting it would be a reasonable assumption that the disease had involved the intestines. This may have been what Clark meant when he said that the seat of Keats's trouble was the stomach. It should be made clear that it has not and now cannot be substantiated that Keats did in fact have abdominal tuberculosis. What is surprising is that Clark, who had a special interest in phthisis, and presumably having been informed of his new patient's family history as well as the diagnosis of the London physicians together with the express purpose of Keats's sojourn in Rome, should come to a conclusion concentrating on stomach and mind rather than the lungs as the major site of the disease."[166]

Sir (Dr.) James Clark

---

[165] Wells, Walter: "*A Doctor's Life of John Keats*", New York: Vantage, 1959, p. 209.
[166] Smith, Hillas: "*Keats and Medicine*", Newport, Isle of Wight: Cross Publishing, 1995), pp. 110–11.

A 2009 biography[167] by Sue Brown of Keats's friend, Joseph Severn, who accompanied him to Italy for treatment of his tuberculosis, published in 2009, once again raises questions about the kind of treatment Keats received from Clark, and claims that the agonies of the poet in the final months in Rome were partly the result of his doctor's misdiagnoses. According to Brown, when Keats arrived in Rome from London in November of 1820, Clark initially was of the opinion that *"mental exertions and application"* were the sources of his complaints which seemed mainly *"situated in his stomach"*. He was of the opinion that if his mind could be put at ease, he would recover.

Finally, after almost a month, when Clark diagnosed tuberculosis, it was already delayed; to make matters worse, the doctor put Keats on a starvation diet of just an anchovy[168] and a piece of bread a day to cut the flow of blood to his stomach.

> *"You cannot think how dreadful this is for me,"* Severn wrote to a friend. *"The Doctor on the one hand tells me I shall kill him to give him more than he allows – and Keats raves till I am in a complete tremble for him."*

Clark also recommended heavy bleeding. On the morning of 9 December, when Keats woke and vomited two cups of blood, he bled his patient, taking away eight further ounces of blood.

Thus, "Keats's doctor", according to Brown, "[…] *didn't treat him very well.*" It was all, according to her, due to medical ignorance. The bleeding pulled the patient right down, and then the near starvation also did irreparable harm to him.

> *"There were times when Keats was hallucinating for lack of oxygen and lack of sustenance,"* Severn wrote to his friends, "[his] *mind is worse than all – despair in every shape – his imagination – and memory present every image in horror so strong that morning and night I tremble for his Intellect ... How he can be Keats again from all this I have little hope."*

---

[167] Brown, Sue: *"Joseph Severn, a Life: The Rewards of Friendship"*, Oxford: Oxford University Press, 2009.

[168] Anchovies are small saltwater fish; anchovies don't get much larger than 7 inches in length. They're also used as bait. It is strongly flavoured and is usually preserved in salt and oil.

The worst of all perhaps was the lack of painkillers given to the poet. Opium in small doses could have, to an extent, relieved his pain. Keats had asked Severn to buy a bottle of opium when they were setting off on their voyage to Rome. It was something Keats wished to keep handy possibly, in extreme case, if he would like to commit suicide. He tried to get the bottle from Severn on the voyage but Severn didn't let him have it. *"Then in Rome he tried again,"* writes Brown in the biography, *"Severn was in such a quandary he didn't know what to do, so in the end he went to the doctor who took it away. As a result Keats went through dreadful agonies with nothing to ease the pain at all."*

Keats was furious for being denied opium, throwing two cups of coffee at Severn and later turning his anger on Clark, asking the doctor whenever he appeared: *"how long is this posthumous existence of mine to go on"*.[169]

According to Brown, the tragedy was that Keats wasn't only suffering through physical anguish, but also with *"mental anguish and emotional anguish"*. At the time of his death, he believed he had been a complete failure as a poet. "It's unbearable really to think about that," she said. Moreover, there "[…] *was also the pain, not of a failed relationship with Fanny Brawne, but of one which could never be consummated."*

"Is the Criticism of John Keats's Doctor Justified? A Bicentenary Re-Appraisal

The controversy over Keats's death has recently been revisited by two eminent doctors, Dr. Sean Patrick Francis Hughes, Emeritus professor of orthopaedic surgery at Imperial College London and Dr. Noel Snell, Director of Research, British Lung Foundation, in a paper published in 2021, the bicentennial of Keats's death.[170] Based on their analysis of the mode of contemporary treatment of consumption that was in practice in the early part of the nineteenth century, they argue that Keats's doctor, Clark, who treated him in Rome, has been unfairly castigated by modern scholars and that he

---

[169] Flood, Alison: "*Doctor's mistakes to blame for Keats's agonising end, says new biography*", The Guardian, 26 Oct 2009.

[170] Hughes, Sean P. & Snell, Noel: ""*Is the Criticism of John Keats's Doctors Justified? A Bicentenary Re-Appraisa*l", Taylor & Francis Online, Published online: 23 Jun 2021, pp. 41-55.

followed the same course of treatment of consumption that was in vogue at that time.

To scrutinize the issue, it has been first sought to ascertain when did Clark come to know that Keats had pulmonary tuberculosis after he saw the poet. Based on the available evidence as well as the letters of the poet and his friends, Hughes & Snell, in their paper, systematically analyse the chronological sequence of events beginning with the onset Keats's illness, and assert that Clark did know that Keats had consumption soon after he saw the patient and believed that it affected both his stomach and lungs, and applied the knowledge then available for the management of consumption; his approach to the treatment of John Keats was, therefore, entirely rational.

As described earlier, on 17 September, 1820 Keats, accompanied by his friend Severn, left for Rome on board the sailing brig Maria Crowther. On 21 October 1820, when they arrived in Naples, Keats was not well and was suffering the effects from the long journey. Severn records that in Naples blood came from Keats's stomach and he had a fever at night and also suffered violent perspiration.[171] The problem was compounded further as the city authorities didn't allow their vessel to enter the port and forced them to remain in quarantine for a period of ten days.

Keats's treatment in Rome

Keats arrived in Rome on 15 November 1820. He had a letter of introduction to Dr Clark.[172] Clark found an accommodation for Keats and Severn in the Piazza di Spagna, adjacent to the Spanish Steps, where they lived on the second floor, and he took over Keats's care treating him from November 1820 to February 1821.

Clark wrote on 27 November 1820,

> *"Keats arrived here about a week ago & I have got him comfortable lodgings. I can hardly yet give you a decided opinion of the case [. .*

---

[171] *"The Keats Circle, Letters and Papers 1816–1878, and More Letters and Poems, 1814–1879"*, ed. Hyder Edward Rollins, 2 vols., Cambridge, MA: Harvard University Press, 1969, I, p. 163.

[172] In fact, there was to be a meeting in London between Keats and Clark before he was to leave England , but somehow it never occurred, and Keats travelled to Italy on 17 September 1820, accompanied by his painter friend Joseph Severn.

> .] *The chief part of his disease, as far as I can yet see seems seated in his Stomach. I have some suspicion of disease of the heart and it may be of the lungs, but of this say nothing to his friends* [. . .] *His mental exertions and application have I think been the sources of his complaints— If I can put his mind at ease I think he'll do well* [. . .] *If my opinion be correct we may throw medicine to the dogs.*[173] *Let everything be done to relieve his mind from any Idea of that kind as far as possible.*"[174]

Therefore, shortly after Keats's arrival in Rome, Clark diagnosed that he was physically ill. He had disease involving his stomach and Clark was suspicious that it was also affecting his heart and lungs, and in addition Keats was suffering from nervous exhaustion.

What did Clark mean when he wrote 'we may throw medicine to the dogs'? Was he implying that Keats had no overwhelming physical illness? Was he really of the opinion that all of Keats's condition was primarily in his mind?

On 30 November 1820, Keats wrote to Charles Brown,

> "'*Tis the most difficult thing in the world for me to write a letter. My stomach continues so bad, that I feel it worse on opening any book,— yet I am much better than I was in quarantine* [. . .] *Dr. Clark is very attentive to me; he says, there is very little the matter with my lungs, but my stomach, he says, is very bad.*"[175]

So, the material question is: Was Clark being entirely honest with Keats about his condition? Why did he say there was little the matter with [Keats's] lungs? Did he think that Keats's condition was too far advanced for there to be any hope of success from medical treatment? According to Hughes and Snell, Clark was being a compassionate doctor, only telling his patient about a possibly treatable condition and hiding his suspicions from Keats that his lungs were affected.

---

[173] Probably as noted by Hyder Rollins, this is a quotation from Shakespeare, Macbeth, V.iii.47, 'Throw physic to the dogs; I'll none of it'. It is not known who the letter was addressed to, although Rollins in Keats Circle suggests it was a Samuel E. Gray.

[174] "*Keats Circle*", ed. Rollins, I, pp. 171–2.

[175] "*Letters of Keats*", ed. Forman, pp. 525–7.

At this stage Severn was also questioning the effect the long journey had on Keats:

> "*I do lament a thousand times that he ever left England—not from the want of medical aid or even friends—for nothing can be superior to the kindness of Dr Clark &c—but the journey of 2000 Miles was too much in his state—even when he left England—and now he has most surely broken down under it.*"[176]

Again on 24 December 1820, Severn wrote to Taylor (Keats's publisher):

> "*Dr Clark gives very little hope of him—he says he may* [re]*cover from* [th]*is by some change in his mind—but he will* [m]*ost certainly die (at some not distant period) of Consumption—* [n]*o disorganisation exists at present—but a total derangement* [of] *the digestive powers— they have nearly lost their functions* [and] *it is this cause that produces the blood from the heads of* [. . .] *on the chest.*"[177]

So, by Christmas 1820 Clark knew Keats was dying from consumption. Showing his concern, he sought the opinion of a local Italian doctor who diagnosed that Keats had a malformed chest. The doctor also commented that should Keats die, the law in Italy demanded that a post-mortem would have to take place.[178]

On 3 January 1821, Clark wrote:

> "*he has had another attack of bleeding from the lungs which has weakened him greatly, and he is now in a most deplorable state.— His stomach is ruined and the state of his mind is the worst possible for one in his condition* [. . .] *His digestive organs are sadly deranged and his lungs are also diseased—either of these would be a great evil, but to have both under the state of mind which he unfortunately is in must soon kill him.*"[179]

---

[176] "*Keats Circle*", ed. Rollins, I, p. 182.
[177] Ibid.
[178] Ibid., p. 184.
[179] Ibid.

In the same letter, Clark also wrote that when he first saw Keats he thought something might be done *'but now I fear the prospect is a hopeless one'*.[180] It is, therefore, clear that by this stage Clark knew Keats was suffering from consumption involving his lungs and digestive system and that he was dying.

On 15 January 1821, Clark wrote a letter to an employee of Taylor's, mainly concerning obtaining money for Keats:

> *"Poor fellow he is now so ill as to be constantly confined to bed, his stomach is still in a very bad state, the affection of his lungs is increasing and the state of his mind is the most deplorable possible."*[181]

With each passing day, Keats's condition worsened, and ultimately he died in Severn's arms at eleven o'clock at night on 23 February 1821.

On 25 February 1821 Clark carried out a post-mortem examination in the company of an Italian doctor, Dr Luby, which Severn records, *"they thought it the worst possible Consumption – the lungs were entirely destroyed – the cells were quite gone"*.[182]

Keats was later buried in the Protestant cemetery in Rome. All his bedding and furniture were burnt (at a cost to Severn of £150), as the Italians believed in the contagious nature of consumption.

Clark's Treatment of Keats: A Critical Analysis

A question that has often been raised concerning Keats's treatment in Rome is why did Clark persist in treating him with bloodletting? René Laennec's exemplary volume on *"Diseases of the Chest"*, published in French in 1819, stated that, apart from a couple of specific indications, *"bleeding ought never to be employed in the treatment of consumption"*.[183] Clark may have been aware of this as it was on his recommendation that Laennec's treatise was translated and published in English. Clark's advocacy of bloodletting, however, was a common practice at that time. In fact, a

---

[180] *"Keats Circle"*, ed. Rollins, I, pp. 185–6. It is not known who this letter was addressed to, but Rollins suggest it was also to Gray.
[181] *"Keats Circle"*, ed. Rollins, I, p. 194.
[182] *"Keats Circle"*, ed. Rollins, I, p. 225.
[183] Laennec, R.: *"A Treatise on the Diseases of the Chest and on Mediate Auscultation"*, 4th edition, London: Longman, 1834, p.331.

discussion on bloodletting published in the Proceedings of the Royal Society of Medicine as late as 1927 showed that it was still quite widely used in some situations. Hence it can be argued that Clark was not acting out of the ordinary in 1820-1 when treating Keats in Rome in the manner he did.

Another question that remains is: Was Keats treated humanely by Clark when he was under his care in Rome? By January 1821 Clark knew Keats had pulmonary consumption and he showed his humanity by caring for him. He visited Keats regularly, his wife bought food for Keats and Severn, and Clark took on responsibility even for obtaining funds, since by this stage Severn was nursing Keats virtually on his own and was unable to earn his living as a portrait painter.

In this context, it is also relevant to refer to Richard Monckton Milnes (1809-1885) who wrote in his *"Letter and Life of John Keats"* that Keats was very ill in Naples and on arriving in Rome,

> *"the attention he received was that of all the skill and knowledge that science could confer [. . .] All that wise solitude and delicate thoughtfulness could do to light up the dark passages of mortal sickness and soothe the pillow of the forlorn stranger was done [. . .] At least from this desolation Keats was saved by the love and care of Mr Severn and Dr Clark."*

From the treatment chart in particular, it is clear that Clark used the standard methods then available in order to manage Keats's consumption. He restricted Keats's diet because of his concern for his gastric dyspepsia believing that the alimentary system needed resting. He advised Keats to undertake exercise, especially horse riding, to improve his wellbeing and perhaps his lung function. Furthermore, he regularly bled Keats in order to reduce his abdominal venous congestion. Clark's letters make it clear he knew Keats had consumption, and that the disorder was advanced by the time he first saw him in November 1820 and then by January 1821 had progressed too far for Clark to manage other than by compassion and empathy.

In view of the above, it is reasonable to conclude that history has been unkind to Dr. Clark's management of John Keats in Rome. What he did to Keats to treat him was according to what were then acceptable standards of medicine, including his advocacy of venesection for treating patients with consumption.[184] Clark's management of consumption of the poet John Keats was appropriate and that he was a caring and concerned doctor.

Was it a prudent decision for Keats to travel all the way to Rome just for a bit of sunshine?

Before we conclude, there is another question we would like to probe, i.e., whether Keats was rightly advised by his doctors in London to do what he did – namely, to undertake such extremely tedious journey to Rome that seriously affected his health, just for a bit of sunshine?

Keats himself was a qualified doctor; so after early recognition of the significance of his episode of haemoptysis, he clearly understood what was wrong with him. In his letter of 20 August 1820 to Charles Brown when he had resolved go to Italy, Keats wrote, *"Not that I have any great hopes of that, for, I think, there is a core of disease in me not easy to pull out"*.[185] In addition, on 22 September 1820, before setting off for Italy, Keats wrote his will and sent it to Taylor, *"In case of my death this scrap of Paper may be of service[e]- able in your possession."*[186] Keats wrote again to Brown on 28 September 1820, just before he sailed: *"The very thing which I want to live most for will be a great occasion of my death. I cannot help it. Who can help it?"*[187]

From these letters it can be inferred that Keats knew he was dying in the summer of 1820, but he took advice to travel abroad as a possible last hope for a cure. The advice he got from his doctors in England to go Italy, however, does not appear to be a sound advice.

---

[184] It should be noted that in more recent times it has been discovered that Mycobacterium tuberculosis requires iron in order to thrive, and bleeding will reduce the body's iron stores, so potentially could be beneficial.

[See, (i) Lounis, Nacer, Caroline Maslo, Johan R. Boelaert, Chantal Truffot-Pernot, Ji Baohong, Jacques Grosset, *"Impact of iron loading and iron chelation on murine tuberculosis,"* Clinical Microbiology and Infection, Vol. 5, No. 11 (1999): pp. 687–92;

(ii) Lounis, Nacer, Chantal Truffot-Pernot, Jacques Grosset, Victor R. Gordeuk, Johan R. Boelaert, *"Iron and Mycobacterium tuberculosis infection,"* Journal of Clinical Virology, Vol. 20 No. 3 (2001): pp. 123–6.

[185] *"Letters of Keats"*, ed. Forman, p. 514.

[186] *"Letters of Keats"*, ed. Forman, p. 511.

[187] *"Letters of Keats"*, ed. Forman, p. 520.

If Clark had met Keats in London before the latter set out for Rome, as had been proposed, would he have advised him to travel to Rome in 1820? The answer to this lies in Severn's letter to Taylor dated 25/26 January 1821, when he wrote that the doctor says Keats should never have left England.[188] In fact, by 1836 when Clark wrote his book on pulmonary consumption he wrote, perhaps remembering Keats, that the medical advisor should hesitate before sending a patient on a long journey in an advanced stage of pulmonary consumption: *"He arrives in worse condition then when he left his own country, and doomed shortly to add another name to the long and melancholy list of his countrymen who have sought, with pain and suffering, a distant country only to find in it a grave."*

---

[188] *"Keats Circle"*, ed. Rollins, I, p. 204.

Chapter 24
Death Mask of John Keats

"Some say the world is a vale of tears, I say it is a place of soul-making."

- John Keats

Death Mask

Keats died of tuberculosis in Rome during the night of 23 February 1821, attended only by his friend, the artist Joseph Severn. After Keats's death, the furniture in his room – now a museum – was burned. The death mask was taken the next day, when 'a gentleman was sent to cast the face, hand and foot'. Severn used these casts for his posthumous full-length portrait of Keats (now in the National Portrait Gallery), which he undertook in an attempt to exorcize the impression of Keats's death which was so painful and to memorialize his friend with '*the most pleasant remembrance.*' By 16 May 1821, Severn had begun to paint a posthumous portrait of Keats reading at Wentworth Place, when John Taylor, Keats's publisher, wrote to him requesting that he send Taylor the casts. Severn replied that "*the casts I must send another time because I still require them to finish the picture from.*" The portrait by Severn, finished about 1822, is thus in part a contemporary depiction of the death mask; it is among the most enduring images of Keats.

For preparing the death mask, Keats's face was shaved and prepared, so a plaster cast could be applied to preserve his likeness. In the death mask the poet's lips and eyes are expressionless and, after years of illness, he has a thinner nose, slightly more hollowed cheeks and more pronounced infraorbital edema beneath his eyes.

Now, more than 200 years after his death, two versions of Keats's death mask produced by two cast makers circulate galleries, auctions and private collections for large sums. Their value is a testament to Keats's enduring appeal. Recently, in December 2021, Adeline Johns-Putra, a professor of literature specialising in British Romanticism, bought a death mask of John Keats, produced by Charles Smith and Sons, at a price of £12,500 in an online Christie's auction.

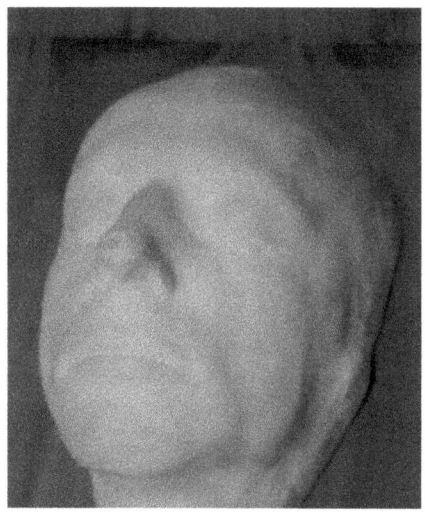

Death Mask of John Keats
(This is one of a series of white plaster casts
made by Charles Smith between 1886 and 1891.)

Peter Malone spent more than a decade tracing the history of Keats's death masks, after discovering one in the window of a second-hand bookshop in 2001. That copies of the mask eventually reappeared is a sign of its worth, he says: "*For the mask to spend 80 years in the dark means that someone valued it and knew its identity, otherwise it would have gone the way of most plaster.*"

A careful study[189] of the death mask by Peter Malone reveals that two masks were made from the original mould in 1821. One was kept by artist Joseph Severn, who used the resemblance to paint a posthumous portrait of Keats. The other went to Keats's publisher, John Taylor, in London. Both of these were lost – but a few of the death masks produced by Charles Smith and Sons in London,[190] which made several casts of the mask around 1898 to 1905, still survive. According to Malone, these are decidedly superior and

---

[189] Malone, Peter: '*Keats's "Posthumous Existence" in Plaster*', The Keats-Shelley Review, vol. 26, 2012, pp.125-35.

[190] The death mask purchased by Johns-Putra, in December 2021, was produced by Charles Smith and Sons,

are inscribed with Smith's name at the crown with his inventory number 231 and the poet's name at the throat. Christie's now estimates that there are only nine Smith casts remaining.

The second modern source of Keats's death mask was the Parisian cast making firm Lorenzi, which continues to make copies using a rubber mould. It is unclear how many Lorenzis are in circulation; however, as these masks lack the inscription "Keats" on the throat (visible on the Smith cast), they are not as highly prized. It is no. 921 in their catalogue, and as they lack Keats name, Malone has found that casts from this mould have been misidentified as Baudelaire, Napoleon I and the astronomer Le Verrier.

Life Mask of John Keats

Keats also had a life mask made in 1816, five years before his death, allowing us to observe how the wasting disease affected the poet's appearance. *"The nose is more aquiline in the death mask. I would say that the cheeks are a bit more sunken. I think the bone structure's a bit more evident. These are rather to be expected,"* Malone says. *"Some people probably think it's a little bit morbid, but I think it is a very beautiful object."*[191]

Benjamin Haydon

---

[191] Lloyd, Andrew: *"Writ in water, preserved in plaster: how Keats' death mask became a collector's item"*, The Guardian, 26 Feb 2021.

The renowned British painter Benjamin Robert Haydon first met Keats on 19th October 1816 and the two became good friends. Haydon asked if he could include Keats as one of the onlookers in his massive painting *"Christ's Entry into Jerusalem"* (now in the collection of The Athenaeum of Ohio, Cincinnati, Ohio, USA). For this purpose, he made the original life mask of John Keats so that he could draw from it without the latter having to sit for hours. The cast was made on Saturday 14th December 1816. Keats's hair was held back by a band, he then lay on his back while his face was greased with fat and straws stuck up his nose so that he could breathe while Haydon covered his face with Plaster of Paris. This was then left to set before being peeled off and then finished by hand. In this way a negative mould of Keats's face was made, from which positive casts could be made.

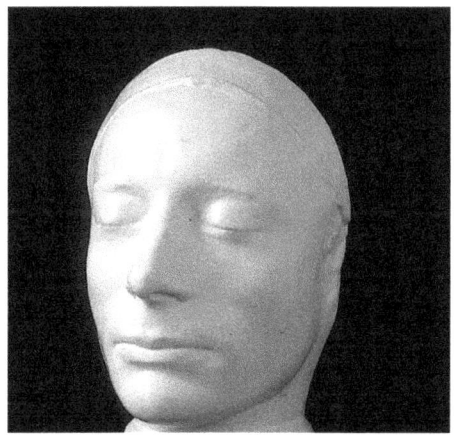

A life mask of John Keats,
(The original made by Benjamin Haydon)

Keats's face is serene but there is, perhaps, a noticeable smile on his lips. Sitting for the mask would probably have been quite amusing though uncomfortable. There is therefore, in this life mask, a more animated sense of the subject's character than in a death mask taken from the deceased subject. Here he has a serene stillness: the viewer can sense the contemplative composure observed during the period of the plaster setting. In the words of Fanny Keats (Keats's sister), Haydon's mask was *"a perfect copy of the features of my dear brother. The expression of course is wanting as the eyes are closed, and perhaps the mouth is a little compressed which is but natural, as the mask could not have been taken with the lips unclosed. It is perfect, except for the mouth, the lips being rather thicker and somewhat compressed which renders the expression more severe than the sweet and mild original.*"

By the mid-19th-century a matrix taken from an original cast of the Life Mask had come into the possession of the Brucciani firm of cast-makers who subsequently issued copies from it. The Brucciani matrix was acquired by the V&A casting service in the 1920s and subsequently transferred to the British Museum in the early 1980s.[192]

---

[192] "*John Keats (1795-1821), Life Mask by Benjamin Robert Haydon (1786-1846)*", TREGEAGLE. https://shorturl.at/acAJW

Chapter 25
Burial

"Mist to mist, drops to drops. For water thou art, and unto water shalt thou return."

- Kamand Kojouri[193]

Keats breathed his last on Friday the 23 February, at about eleven in the night. Three days later, on Monday 26 February, he was buried just before dawn in the Protestant Cemetery, Rome. Several of Fanny's unread letters were buried with him.[194]

Grave of John Keats, Protestant Cemetery, Rome

---

[193] Born in Tehran, raised in Dubai and Toronto, Kamand Kojouri currently resides in England. She is a poet, and author of *"The Eternal Dance: Love Poetry and Prose"* and *"God, Does Humanity Exist?"*. With every book sold (paperback, eBook, or Audiobook), Kamand donates to have a tree planted in Sub-Saharan Africa to help provide families with food, income, and a sustainable way of life.

[194] Walsh, John Evangelist. *"Darkling, I Listen: The Last Days and Death of John Keats"*, New York: St. Martin's Press, 1999.

The inscription on the headstone of Keats's tomb reads,

> *"This Grave*
> *contains all that was Mortal*
> *of a*
> *Young English Poet,*
> *Who,*
> *on his Death Bed,*
> *in the Bitterness of his Heart,*
> *at the Malicious Power of his Enemies,*
> *Desired*
> *these Words to be engraven on his Tomb Stone:*
> *HERE LIES ONE WHOSE NAME WAS WRIT IN*
> *WATER.*
> *th*
> *Feb 24 1821"*

Above the inscription is an image of a lyre, symbol of Apollo, the Greek and Roman god of poetry. The missing strings symbolise a life cut short.

As the tombstone points out, Keats desired only the phrase *"Here lies one whose name was writ in water"* inscribed on his tombstone. He did not even want his name to appear on his tombstone; merely this line. The rest of the inscription was added by his friend Severn, who nursed him during his illness, and Keats's closest friend, Charles Brown. Both were grief-stricken and embittered by the critical treatment of Keats's poetry by a section of contemporary critics.[195]

---

[195] Years later both were to admit regret for the epitaph. Severn wrote on July 13th, 1836 "*…the present gravestone with its inscription is an eyesore to me and more…*" while Brown referred to it as "*…a sort of profanation…*" (6) . These belated pangs of regret help to establish the view that the epitaph was not what Keats wanted. [Source: Reynolds, Ian: "*The Gravestone of John Keats: Romancing the Stone*", Wordsworth Grasmere, 16 April, 2018]. https://shorturl.at/fyCTU

James Clark, his attending doctor in Rome, saw to the planting of daisies on the grave, saying that Keats would have wished it.

Adonais

After Keats died in February 1821, the grief over Keats's death and the savage criticism of his poetry by a section of critics incited Shelley to write a remarkable and classically-inspired Miltonic elegy on Keats, "*Adonais*" in April (published in July). The elegy was patterned on Bion's lament for Adonais, and after showing the muses, the seasons, the dreams, the desires, the pleasures, and the sorrows - all weeping at the bier, rises "*to a triumphant declaration of the poet's immortality*".

"Adonais"

I

"I weep for Adonais—he is dead!
Oh, weep for Adonais! Though our tears
Thaw not the frost which binds so dear a head!
And thou, sad Hour, selected from all years
To mourn our loss, rouse thy obscure compeers,
And teach them thine own sorrow, say: "With me
Died Adonais; till the Future dares
Forget the Past, his fate and fame shall be
An echo and a light unto eternity!"

II

Where wert thou, mighty Mother, when he lay,
When thy Son lay, pierc'd by the shaft which flies
In darkness? Where was lorn Urania
When Adonais died? With veiled eyes,
'Mid listening Echoes, in her Paradise
She sate, while one, with soft enamour'd breath,
Rekindled all the fading melodies,
With which, like flowers that mock the corse beneath,
He had adorn'd and hid the coming bulk of Death

> **III**
>
> *Oh, weep for Adonais—he is dead!*
> *Wake, melancholy Mother, wake and weep!*
> *Yet wherefore? Quench within their burning bed*
> *Thy fiery tears, and let thy loud heart keep*
> *Like his, a mute and uncomplaining sleep;*
> *For he is gone, where all things wise and fair*
> *Descend—oh, dream not that the amorous Deep*
> *Will yet restore him to the vital air;*
> *Death feeds on his mute voice, and laughs at our despair. …"*

The poem "*Adonais*" elevates Keats's status while also fashioning him as the sensitive victim of malevolent reviewers; this sticks to Keats's reputation well into the nineteenth century, though Shelley is not the first to sound the sentiment; in fact, it is right there on Keats's gravestone.

On July 8 the following year, Shelley was drowned on his way from Leghorn to Lerici. He was also buried in the same Protestant Cemetery, Rome, where Keats is buried. At the time of his death, Shelley was carrying in his pocket the manuscript of his "*The Indian Serenade*", the poems of Sophocles and of his dear friend, John Keats.[196]

---

[196] Schuster, M. Lincoln: "*The World's Great Letters*", Simon & Schuster Inc. New York City, New York, 1940, p.242.

Grave of Percy Bysshe Shelley, Protestant Cemetery, Rome

Grave of John Keats and Joseph Severn, Protestant Cemetery, Rome

Severn died on 3 August 1879 at the age of 85, and was buried in the same Cemetery next to Keats with an inscription identifying him as the "*devoted friend and death-bed companion of John Keats, whom he lived to see numbered among the Immortal Poets of England.*". Both gravestones are still standing today side by side.

Chapter 26
The Tomb of John Keats: Through the eyes of Oscar Wilde (1877)

"In my heaven he walks eternally with Shakespeare and the Greeks."

-- Oscar Wilde on 'John Keats

'Irish Monthly', July 5, 1877: "The Tomb of John Keats"

In July 1877, subscribers to the *'Irish Monthly'*, a publication subtitled *'A Magazine of General Literature'*, were treated to an entertaining and scholarly article headed *'The Tomb of John Keats'*. The author, a 22-year-old Dubliner, was an undergraduate at Magdalen College, Oxford, where he was reading Literae Humaniores, the university's undergraduate course in Classics. This was his first published prose article and his name was Oscar Wilde.

In this moving tribute to the young poet, which can be read here, Wilde, an avid fan, introduced Keats as *'one who walks with Spenser, and Shakespeare, and Byron, and Shelley, and Elizabeth Barrett Browning in the great procession of the sweet singers of England'*. While allowing that the resting place of *'this divine boy'*, which he had visited earlier that year, was surrounded by beauty, Wilde insisted that Keats's brief but extraordinary life was not honoured fittingly by the *'mean grave'* that held his remains. Describing the emotions that came over him as he stood by Keats's graveside, Wilde paid florid homage to his hero: *'I thought of him as of a Priest of Beauty slain before his time; and the vision of Guido's St. Sebastian came before my eyes as I saw him at Genoa'*. For the sake of fuller appreciation of Wilde's glorious tribute to Keats, his 1877-artcle published in *'Irish Monthly'* is reproduced below:

"The Tomb of John Keats
By Oscar Wilde
(Irish Monthly, July 5, 1877)

As one enters Rome from the Via Ostiensis by the Porta San Paolo, the first object that meets the eye is a marble pyramid which stands close at hand on the left.

There are many Egyptian obelisks in Rome–tall, snakelike spires of red sandstone, mottled with strange writings, which remind us of the pillars of flame which led the children of Israel through the desert away from the land of the Pharaohs; but more wonderful than these to look upon is this gaunt, wedge-shaped pyramid standing here in this Italian city, unshattered amid the ruins and wrecks of time, looking older than the Eternal City itself, like terrible impassiveness turned to stone. And so in the Middle Ages men supposed this to be the sepulchre of Remus, who was slain by his own brother at the founding of the city, so ancient and mysterious it appears; but we have now, perhaps unfortunately, more accurate information about it, and know that it is the tomb of one Caius Cestius, a Roman gentleman of small note, who died about 30 B.C.

Yet though we cannot care much for the dead man who lies in lonely state beneath it, and who is only known to the world through his sepulchre, still this pyramid will be ever dear to the eyes of all English-speaking people, because at evening its shadows fall on the tomb of one who walks with Spenser, and Shakespeare, and Byron, and Shelley, and Elizabeth Barrett Browning in the great procession of the sweet singers of England. For at its foot there is a green, sunny slope, known as the Old Protestant Cemetery, and on this a common-looking grave, which bears the following inscription:

"This Grave

contains all that was Mortal

of a

Young English Poet,

Who,

on his Death Bed,

in the Bitterness of his Heart,

at the Malicious Power of his Enemies,

Desired

these Words to be engraven on his Tomb Stone:
HERE LIES ONE WHOSE NAME WAS WRIT IN WATER.

Feb 24$^{\underline{th}}$ 1821"

And the name of the young English poet is John Keats.

Lord Houghton calls this cemetery 'one of the most beautiful spots on which the eye and heart of man can rest,' and Shelley speaks of it as making one 'in love with death, to think that one should be buried in so sweet a place'; and indeed when I saw the violets and the daisies and the poppies that overgrow the tomb, I remembered how the dead poet had once told his friend that he thought the 'intensest pleasure he had received in life was in watching the growth of flowers,' and how another time, after lying a while quite still, he murmured in some strange prescience of early death, 'I feel the flowers growing over me.'

But this time-worn stone and these wildflowers are but poor memorials of one so great as Keats; most of all, too, in this city of Rome, which pays such honour to her dead; where popes, and emperors, and saints, and cardinals lie hidden in 'porphyry wombs,' or couched in baths of jasper and chalcedony and malachite, ablaze with precious stones and metals, and tended with continual service. For very noble is the site, and worthy of a noble monument; behind looms the grey pyramid, symbol of the world's age, and filled with memories of the sphinx, and the lotus leaf, and the glories of old Nile; in front is the Monte Testaccio, built, it is said, with the broken fragments of the vessels in which all the nations of the East and the West brought their tribute to Rome; and a little distance off, along the slope of the hill under the Aurelian wall, some tall gaunt cypresses rise, like burnt-out funeral torches, to mark the spot where Shelley's heart (that 'heart of hearts'!) lies in the earth; and, above all, the soil on which we tread is very Rome!

As I stood beside the mean grave of this divine boy, I thought of him as of a Priest of Beauty slain before his time; and the vision of Guido's St. Sebastian came before my eyes as I saw him at Genoa, a lovely brown boy, with crisp, clustering hair and red lips, bound by his evil enemies to a tree, and though pierced by arrows, raising his eyes with divine, impassioned gaze towards the Eternal Beauty of the opening heavens. And thus my thoughts shaped themselves to rhyme:

HEU MISERANDE PUER*[197]*(Hello, Poor Boy)

"Rid of the world's injustice and its pain,
He rests at last beneath God's veil of blue;
Taken from life while life and love were new
The youngest of the martyrs here is lain,
Fair as Sebastian and as foully slain.
No cypress shades his grave, nor funeral yew,
But red-lipped daisies, violets drenched with dew,
And sleepy poppies, catch the evening rain.
O proudest heart that broke for misery!
O saddest poet that the world hath seen!
O sweetest singer of the English land!
Thy name was writ in water on the sand,
But our tears shall keep thy memory green,
And make it flourish like a Basil-tree."

Borne, 1877.

[Footnote: {1} Reverently some well-meaning persons have placed a marble slab on the wall of the cemetery with a medallion-profile of Keats on it and some mediocre lines of poetry. The face is ugly, and rather hatchet-shaped,

---

[197] Note: "HEU MISERANDE PUER" ('Hello, Poor Boy') This sonnet was later renamed "*The Grave of Keats*" and included in 'Poems', 1881, p.157

with thick sensual lips, and is utterly unlike the poet himself, who was very beautiful to look upon. '*His countenance,*' says a lady who saw him at one of Hazlitt's lectures, '*lives in my mind as one of singular beauty and brightness; it had the expression as if he had been looking on some glorious sight.*' And this is the idea which Severn's picture of him gives. Even Haydon's rough pen-and-ink sketch of him is better than this '*marble libel,*' which I hope will soon be taken down. I think the best representation of the poet would be a coloured bust, like that of the young Rajah of Koolapoor at Florence, which is a lovely and lifelike work of art.] [198]

---

[198] Fitzsimons, Eleanor: "*Wilde About Keats*", Wordsworth Grasmere, 29 October, 2015. https://shorturl.at/afp18

Chapter 27
Fanny learns of Keats's death

"Shed no tear – O, shed no tear!
The flower will bloom another year.
Weep no more – O, weep no more!
Young buds sleep in the root's white core.
Dry your eyes! oh, dry your eyes!
For I was taught in Paradise
To ease my breast of melodies,—
Shed no tear."
Overhead! look overhead!
'Mong the blossoms white and red--
Look up, look up! I flutter now
On this fresh pomegranate bough.
See me! 'tis this silvery bill
Ever cures the good man's ill.
Shed no tear! oh, shed no tear!
The flower will bloom another year.
Adieu, adieu -- I fly -- adieu!
I vanish in the heaven's blue,--
Adieu, adieu!"

-- John Keats, "Fairy's Song"[199]

It took about three weeks for the news of Keats's death to reach London. A letter from Severn reached Hampstead about April 16, and Fanny learned how the Italian health authorities had burned the furniture in Keats's room, scraped the walls and made new windows and doors and floor. She

---

[199] *"Shed No Tear!"* is one of two *"Fairy Songs"* that appeared in his *"Life, Letters"* (1848).

read of the post mortem and the funeral and how Dr. Clark, Keats's physician in Rome, had made the men plant daisies on the grave, saying that Keats would have wished it.

After hearing news of Keats's death, Fanny soon fell ill and went into mourning; she was grief-stricken but patient – resigned, very resigned. She cut her hair short, donned black clothing as if she had been married to Keats, and wore the ring Keats had given her. She would spend hours in her room re-reading his letters or wandering alone on Hampstead Heath. Unknown to her family, slowly and with much agony she copied the account of his last days; she did not seal it because Keats's sister, Frances, who was barely seventeen then, might want to read it – but she could not read it again. Fanny felt that the only person with whom she could share her grief was Frances with whom she remained in regular correspondence even after Keats's death.

Two years after Keats's death, Fanny started translating short stories from German and publishing them in various magazines. About this time, Keats's sister, Frances, also having come of age, left the Abbeys and went to live with the Brawnes, where she was warmly welcomed.

Fanny came out of mourning in 1827, six years after Keats's death. In 1829, Fanny's mother died at the house at Hampstead. Fanny though sufficiently well off feared a solitary future. She went to live in France, and at Boulogne met young Louis Lindo (afterwards changed to 'Lindon'), scion of a wealthy merchant and banking family of Spanish descent. In 1833, more than 12 years after Keats's death, she married Louis Lindon. She, however, would wear the engagement ring Keats had given her until she died in 1865.

Fanny was thirty-three years of age, her husband twenty-one – when they married. It was not until seven or eight years since they had first met that by accident Louis Lindon became aware of John Keats in her former life; she explained the matter to him though she left him with *"a very imperfect idea of the real case."*

Fanny had three children – two sons, Edmund and Herbert, and one daughter Margaret who was born in Heidelberg, where they had gone to live. It was there she met Thomas Medwin, a cousin and biographer of the great Romantic poet Percy Bysshe Shelley. She collaborated with him to correct a wrong notion that Keats had gone insane in his final days. The impression was caused by Shelly's wife and the author of "Frankenstein",

Mary Shelley, in her edited volume *"Essays, Letters from Abroad, Translations and Fragments"* (1840). Fanny showed letters to Medwin that suggested otherwise. Medwin used this new information in his *"Life of Shelley"* (1847), where he published extracts from these letters by Keats himself and his friend Joseph Severn.[200]

Keats was barely 25 years old and largely unknown when he died. In the years following his death, his genius was recognised; his works sold briskly. In 1848, the first biography of Keats by Richard Monckton Milnes was published. Over the years, he came to be recognised among the greatest English poets.

Fanny had witnessed the growth of Keats's reputation; she must have had read the numerous books that eulogized him. But she never revealed herself. In 1829, she granted permission to Charles Brown to reproduce for biographical purposes some letters and poems of Keats's concerning his relationship with her – but without using her name. Later after her marriage, her husband knew only that she and the poet had met as neighbours in Hampstead. Fanny never told him anything more. Also, unknown to her husband, she had kept Keats's love letters to her, over three dozen of them; many were mere notes, several lengthy chronicles of his devotion, others jealous ramblings which revealed many innate facets of the poet's character.

In 1859, after many years abroad, Fanny's family (now Mrs. Lindon) returned to England and settled in Pimlico. Their comfortable years was over; and to help her husband through his money troubles, Fanny sold, much against her wishes, her miniature of Keats to Sir Charles Dilke.

In the autumn of 1865, Fanny told her children about her affairs with Keats and entrusted to them the relics of their romance, including his books and the letters Keats had written to her, which she told them would *"someday be considered of value"*. She also made them promise never to tell their father.

---

[200] Lovell Jr., Ernest J: *"Captain Medwin: Friend of Byron and Shelley"*, University of Texas, 1962.

Fanny Brawne's Grave at Brompton Cemetery, London

On 4 December 1865, Fanny Brawne died and was buried the next day in Brompton Cemetery in London.[201]

---

[201] Richardson, Joanna: *"Fanny Brawne, a biography"*, Thames & Hudson, 1952

Chapter 28
1885: Sale by auction of Keats's love-letters

"You are always new. The last of your kisses was even the sweetest; the last smile the brightest; the last movement the gracefullest."

-- John Keats

December 8, 1865: London Times, Front page

On 8 December 1865, the front page of the London Times included the following obituary:

> *"On the 4 inst., at 34 Coleshill-street, Eaton-square,*
>
> *Frances, the wife of Louis Lindon, Esq.*
>
> *Friends will kindly accept this intimation."*
>
> *The 65 year old Mrs Lindon was survived by her husband, a sales agent twelve years her junior, and three children. The eldest, 31 year old Edmund was in government service; 27 year old Herbert and 21 year old Margaret still lived at home. Their mother's death naturally affected them, but it was otherwise of interest only to those with memories of Hampstead forty-six years ago. For it was there, in the autumn of 1818, that Frances Lindon had been known as Fanny Brawne. And it was there that she met a struggling young poet named John Keats. The anonymous Mrs Lindon was, in fact, the mysterious, unnamed beloved of the now famous Keats."*

Fanny was little known among the public at large during her lifetime. And so, in 1865, at the time of her demise, no one would as such consider the death of a 65 year old Frances Lindon to be noteworthy; but she was considered worthy of mention in newspapers as the beloved of John Keats who had by then been recognised as one of the greatest English poets of the Romantic era.

Water colour miniature of Fanny Brawne
at Keats House Museum, Hampstead, London

It was years after her death the romance between Keats and Fanny became a widely known affair when her children decided to sell the love letters. She had told her children of her romance with Keats, and had shown them her collection of his books and love letters; but she had also made them promise never to tell their father.

Fanny's children Herbert and Margaret Lindon kept their promise and maintained the secret till their father Louis Lindon was alive. Seven years later, after the demise of their father on 21 October, 1872, Fanny's children (led primarily by Herbert) set about looking for potential buyers of their mother's relics. They decided to publish the letters in book form and auction them some time after. Accordingly, in February 1878, a slim, elegantly designed volume titled *"Letters of John Keats to Fanny Brawne"* edited by Harry Buxton Forman, was published. It was the first time the public had heard of Fanny Brawne, and it aroused a great deal of interest among literary scholars. The publication of Keats's love letters to Fanny caused much interest in England and America. Subsequently, on 2 March 1885, thirty-five of Keats's love letters to Fanny Brawne were sold by her son Herbert Lindon at an auction in the rooms of Sotheby, Wilkinson and Hodge in London for £543 17s.

Love made public

As the love letters of Keats to Fanny were personal and intimate, there was a major controversy over publication of the letters. In response to his attackers, the editor of the publication, H. B. Forman, defended his action saying that Keats's letters without those to Fanny Brawne were very much like 'Hamlet' without the Prince of Denmark. The sense of outrage at the violation of the poet's privacy, however, did not die down quickly.

Among those present at the auction of Keats's love letters on March 2, 1885 was Oscar Wilde, who bid with the rest and despite his apparent distaste, he purchased one (out of thirty-five love letters put to auction) for himself for eighteen pounds. As one not at all pleased over the sale of Keats's love letters by auction, he wrote:

Oscar Wilde

"On The Sale By Auction Of Keats's Love Letters"

"These are the letters which Endymion wrote
To one he loved in secret, and apart,
And now the brawlers of the auction mart
Bargained and bid for each poor blotted note,
Ay, for each separate pulse of passion quote
The latest price – I think they love not Art
Who break the crystal of a poet's heart

> *That small and sickly eyes may glare or gloat.*
> *Is it not said, that many years ago*
> *In a far Eastern Town some soldiers ran*
> *With torches through the midnight, and began*
> *To wrangle for mean raiment, and to throw*
> *Dice for the garments of a wretched man,*
> *Not knowing the God's wonder or His woe?*
>
> [Oscar Wilde, *"On the Sale by Auction of Keats's Love-Letters"*][202][203]

Ironically, ten years later, when Wilde was imprisoned on the charges of homosexuality, he too suffered the same fate. His precious literary (and other) belongings were auctioned cheaply at his ransacked home. Included in the sale was a lot listed as *'a Manuscript Poem by Keats, framed'* sold off for 38 shillings. Interestingly, this was the original manuscript of Keats's *'Sonnet on Blue'*[204] given to Wilde by Keats's niece Emma Speed, daughter of Keats's brother George who had emigrated to America in 1818 before settling in Louisville a year later.

Mrs. Speed and Wilde came to know each other when Wilde visited Louisville, Kentucky on his American lecture tour of 1882, and included in his talk a reference to Keats's *Sonnet on Blue*. By a happy chance in the audience that night, to listen to Wilde, was Keats's niece Emma Speed. Following Wilde's lecture, Mrs Speed and Wilde were introduced and they arranged to meet the next day at her home at 616 First Street, in Louisville. As Wilde recalled:

---

[202] Schuster, M. Lincoln, *"The World's Great Letters"*, Simon & Schuster, New York, 1940, p. 248.

[203] Wright, Brooks: "*On the Sale by Auction of Keats's Love Letters*": *A Footnote to Wilde's Sonnet*, Keats-Shelley Journal, Vol. 7 (Winter, 1958), p. 9-11.

[204] The nomenclature *'Sonnet in Blue'* is referential, not an actual title. The allusion is to the poem's opening word and its subject which is the colour of the sea and the sky. The actual poem goes by the name Answer to a Sonnet Ending Thus:-, meaning a response to another sonnet by J. H. Reynolds ending: "*Dark eyes are dearer far/Than those that mock the hyacinthine bell.*"

> *"When my lecture was concluded there came round to see me a lady of middle age, with a sweet gentle manner and a most musical voice. She introduced herself to me as Mrs. Speed, the daughter of George Keats, and invited me to come and examine the Keats manuscripts in her possession. I spent most of the next day with her, reading the letters of Keats to her father, some of which were at that time unpublished, poring over torn yellow leaves and faded scraps of paper, and wondering at the little Dante in which Keats had written those marvellous notes on Milton."*

A few weeks later, as his tour continued, Wilde received a surprise letter from Mrs Speed asking him to accept the original manuscript of the Keats sonnet. Wilde was overcome with emotion and gratitude. He wrote back to her from Omaha, Nebraska:

> *"What you have given me is more golden than gold, more precious than any treasure this great country could yield me......I am half enamoured of the paper that touched his hand, and the ink that did his bidding, grown fond of the sweet comeliness of his character, for since my boyhood I have loved none better than your marvellous kinsman, that godlike boy, the real Adonis of our age.... In my heaven he walks eternally with Shakespeare and the Greeks...."*

Wilde treasured and hung it proudly on the wall of his study. Unfortunately, its present whereabouts are unknown.

So memorable was the episode for Wilde that he later wrote an account of his experience in an article entitled *'Keats Sonnet on Blue'* that appeared in The Hobby Horse, a quarterly Victorian periodical in England published by the Century Guild of Artists.[205]

....

---

[205] The Hobby Horse: the magazine ran from 1884–1894 and spanned a total of seven volumes and 28 issues. The Wilde article was in the July 1886 issue, pp 83-6. Reprinted in Miscellanies.

Chapter 29
March, 2011: Keats's love letter to Fanny sold at auction for £96, 000.

"The day is gone, and all its sweets are gone!"

\- John Keats

In An Auction Room (Letter of John Keats to Fanny Brawne)
Anderson Galleries, March 15, 1920

To Dr. A.S.W. Rosenbach

"How about this lot? Said the auctioneer;
One hundred, may I say, just for a start?
Between the plum-red curtains, drawn apart,
A written sheet was held [...] And strange to hear
(Dealer, would I were steadfast as thou art)
The cold quick bids. (Against you in the rear)
The crimson salon, in a glow more clear
Burned Bloodlike purple as the poet's heart.
Song that outgrew the singer! Bitter Love
That broke the proud hot heart it held in thrall ---
Poor script, where still those tragic passions move ----
Eight hundred bid, fair warning; the last call;
The soul of Adonais, like a star ....
Sold for eight hundred dollars ---- Doctor R!"

[Christopher Morley][206]

---

[206] Mondlin, Marvin & Meador, Roy: "*Book Row: An Anecdotal & Pictorial History*", Carroll & Graf Publishers, 2004.

About a decade ago, in March, 2011, a love letter written possibly on March 1, 1820 by Keats to Fanny Brawne was auctioned for £96,000. It was the last of Keats's 30 surviving love-letters to Brawne still in private hands. The sale set a world record for a document by the poet. The City of London Corporation bought the letter at Bonhams with the support of the Heritage Lottery Fund.

Confined to sickbed, Keats writes in this letter of his ardent desire to reach out to Fanny but frustrated for he is unable to do so despite living so close to her:[207]

1 (?) March, 1820: *"I shall kiss your name and mine where your Lips have been…"*

> "*My Dearest Fanny,*
>
> *The power of your benediction is not of so weak a nature as to pass from the ring*[208] *in four-and twenty hours --- it is like a sacred Chalice once consecrated and ever consecrate. I shall kiss your name and mine where your Lips have been – Lips! Why should a poor prisoner as I am talk about such things. Thank God, though I hold them the dearest pleasures in the universe, I have a consolation independent of them in the certainty of your affection. I could write a song in the style of Tom Moore's Pathetic about Memory if that would be any relief to me – No. It would not. I will be as obstinate as a Robin. I will not sing in a cage – Health is my expected heaven and you are the Houri – this word I believe is both singular and plural – if only plural, never mind --- you are a thousand of them.*
>
> > *Ever yours affectionately*
> >
> > *my dearest,*
> >
> > *J. K.*

---

[207] Keats, John: "*The complete poetical works and letters of John Keats*", Cambridge Edition, Boston and New York, Houghton, Mifflin and Company, The University Press, Cambridge, 1899, p. 430.

[208] *The ring that Keats refers to was "a seal ring, of agate or cornelian" with "their joint names…engraved upon it."

The letter carried a poignant note on the outer leaf: *"You had better not come today"*

Already ill with the tuberculosis that would kill him a year later, Keats added that forlorn postscript on the envelope: *"You had better not come today."* This last line –scrawled by Keats appeared in *"Bright Star"*, the 2009 film directed by Jane Campion, which dramatized the love affair between Keats and Fanny.

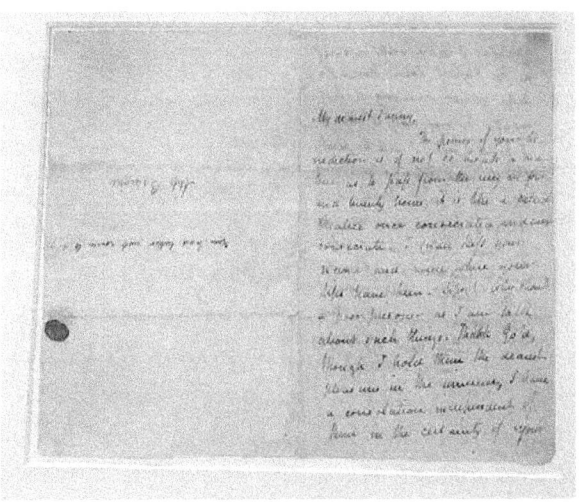

Letter bought by City of London Corporation in March, 2011, Keats House Museum, Hampstead, London

The letter bought through auction by the City of London Corporation in 2011 is currently on display at Keats House Museum, Keats Grove, Hampstead, London where the poet lived from 1818 until 1820. [209]

---

[209] Of the 39 surviving letters written by Keats (in his own hand) to fiancée Brawne (a sliver of the hundreds of notes and letters it is believed he wrote to her), this was the only letter hitherto privately owned. The other letters were already in museums, and also available in published books on the subject.

Chapter 30
Fanny Brawne: Posthumous controversy

"Where are the songs of Spring? Aye, where are they?
Think not of them; thou has thy music too."

-- **John Keats**

In the final year of Keats's short life, he and Fanny remained devoted to each other. In fact, for a month or two prior to Keats's departure to Italy in September 1820, changes in his living situation resulted in Keats's dwelling with the Brawne family, Fanny doing her best to nurse him back to health. Based on surviving letters between the two, Fanny and Keats had fallen even more deeply in love during their last few months together so much so that close friends, particularly Joseph Severn, who accompanied Keats to Rome, also viewed the bond as a detriment worsening Keats' declining health. As Severn wrote while on the ship, *"He was often so distraught, with moreover so sad a look in his eyes, sometimes a starved, haunting expression that it bewildered me."*

Keats's melancholy, as noted by a baffled and concerned Severn, is also revealed in a letter from Keats to another friend named Charles Brown:

"I am afraid to write to her – to receive a letter from her – to see her hand writing would break my heart – even to hear of her anyhow, to see her name written would be more than I could bear…"

Fanny: Unworthy of Keats's affection and love – Critics

After publication of Keats's love letters to Fanny, there was a great deal of interest in Fanny Brawne as a personality; but it also attracted much venom from the critics, who declared her to have been unworthy of Keats's affection and love. Alongside, there was also a perception amongst some that Keats's death on February 23, 1821, shortly after he had left for Rome, was hastened, to a degree, by depression and extreme heartbreak over Fanny. This, in turn, contributed to an unreasoned disaffection for Fanny Brawne.

In a review published in the English literary magazine, "*Athenaeum*", Sir Charles Dilke, the grandson of Keats's friend Dilke, called the compilation of Keats's love letters as *"the greatest impeachment of a woman's sense of womanly delicacy to be found in the history of literature."* In 1890, American poet, essayist and editor Louise Imogen Guiney sardonically remarked that Fanny *"... was vain and shallow, she was almost a child; the gods denied her the 'seeing eye,..."* Seventy years after the poet's death, *"... most of us are soberly thankful that he escaped betimes from his own heart's desire, and his worst impending peril, Mrs. Keats."*

Amongst the critics, the English author and poet Richard Le Gallienne was perhaps the most scathing in his attack; he wrote:

> *"...it is certainly a particularly ironical paradox that the lady irritatingly associated with (Keats's) name should be the least congruous of all the many commonplace women transfigured by the genius they could not understand, and the love of which they were not worthy.... Fame, that loves to humour its poets, has consented to glorify the names of many unimportant poor relations of genius, but there has never been a more significant name upon its lips than the name of Fanny Brawne.... One writes so, remembering... the tortures to which she subjected a noble spirit with her dancing-class coquetries."*

The unsavoury image of Fanny Brawne as portrayed by the critics prevailed for a pretty long time. For several decades, she, *"the girl who shared the fate of John Keats"*, continued to be regarded as a *"lightheaded coquettish minx"* unworthy of love and affection of the great poet.

Fanny Brawne

It was about seventy years after Fanny's death, her letters to Keats's sister, Frances Keats, thirty one in number, came to light that showed her in a more favourable light, greatly improving her reputation. She emerged as an epitome of sincerity and dedication – as one who not only made valiant efforts to save the poet's life, but hoped and waited to marry him; and that she to some extent even appreciated his poetry.

And it all happened, believe it or not, quite dramatically.

Fanny Brawne's letters to Fanny Keats

In 1934, a collector of Keats's works bequeathed his collection of books and Keatsiana to the Keats Memorial House, Hampstead. Interestingly, however, a condition of acceptance imposed by the donor was that the gift should be regarded as anonymous. Included in the gift were the letters that Fanny Brawne had written to Keats's sister, Frances (Fanny) Keats, between September 1820 and June 1824.

Keats had deep affection for his sister, Frances, the youngest of his siblings. **In his last letter dated 30 November, 1820 to his friend Brown, Keats mentioned about Frances ---** "*my sister who walks about my imagination like a ghost --- she is so like Tom.*" Before he left for Rome, Keats had dictated a letter to his sister dated September 11, 1820:

> "*It is not illness that prevents me writing, but as I am recommended to avoid every sort of fatigue I have accepted the assistance of a friend (Fanny Brawne) who I have desired to write to you when I am gone, and to communicate any intelligence she may hear of me.*"

Both letter and signature are in Fanny Brawne's handwriting. The letter was written two days before he left Wentworth Place. Keats never wrote again either to his sister or to Fanny. The letters he received from them were buried with him unopened.

Shortly after Keats had left Wentworth, Fanny – as desired by his love – wrote her first letter to Frances on 18 September, 1820 in which she expressed her pleasure in complying with her lover's wishes that she should write to his sister; her sympathy and compassion for the young and friendless girl of seventeen are evident in the letter; and since then **their constant communication allowed them to develop a close friendship.**

After **Keats's death**, she was devastated; but nevertheless she wrote to Frances consoling her:

> "[…] *I know my Keats is happy, I know my Keats is happy, happier a thousand times than he could have been here, for Fanny, you do not, you never can know how much he has suffered. So much that I do believe, were it in my power I would not bring him back. All that grieves me now is that I was not with him, and so near it as I was[...] All we have to console ourselves with is the great joy he felt that all his misfortunes were at an end.*"

She also invited Frances over to their place to stay for a while to overcome her grief and also advised her she must consider her [Fanny's] mother "*as more than a stranger for your brother loved her very much . . . and had he returned I should have been his wife and he would have lived with us …*"

Fanny Brawne   Fanny Keats

Their intimacy continued even after Keats's death. In autumn 1821, Fanny visited Frances in Walthamstow, where she was in the care of their family guardian, Abbeys. Eventually Fanny shared with "*Keats's sister a little of the literary companionship which she had once known with him.*"

In 1937, Oxford University Press published "The *Letters of Fanny Brawne to Fanny Keats, 1820 -1824*".[210] The letters showed Fanny Brawne in a more favourable light, greatly improving her reputation. Fred Edgcumbe,

---

[210] Edgcumbe, Fred (Ed): "*The Letters of Fanny Brawne to Fanny Keats, 1820-1824*", Oxford University Press, H. Milford, 1936.

editor of the volume and curator of the Keats Memorial House, commented in his introduction that *"Those who believed in Fanny Brawne's devotion to Keats have the satisfaction of knowing that their faith has at last been justified."*

Fanny's letters to Frances revealed her deep love for Keats and the determination that no one shall share him – his Keats – with her; *"I have not mentioned your brother."* She wrote to Frances *"To no one but you would I mention him . . . but I can tell you who next to me (I must say next to me) loved him best, that I have not got over it and never shall."* This attitude she maintained, and so when some nine years later Brown wrote to her asking her permission to use letters and poems addressed to her in a projected life of the poet, the same reluctance is reflected in her reply.

Following publication of her letters to Frances, the image of Fanny Brawne underwent a radical change. In sharp contrast with her image painted by some quarters of a vain, shallow, lightheaded girl whom the *"the gods denied the 'seeing eye"*--- unworthy of Keats's affection and love --- these letters brought out a Fanny Brawne hitherto unknown; her understanding and appreciation of literature and art as reflected in the letters by way of her remarks on the books she had read and the pictures she had seen portrayed her, who was only about twenty years of age, as *"a young woman of remarkable perception and imagination, keen in the observance of character and events, possessing an unusual critical faculty, and intellectually fitted to become the wife of Keats."*

In the light of the new revelation, several of those who were highly critical of her earlier changed their views. After reviewing his own assessment about her twenty-five years before, John Middleton Murry, a leading critic of the time, said *"I have seized the opportunity of considering anew the character of Fanny Brawne and the nature of her influence on Keats. ...I have had the deep satisfaction of being able completely to recant the harsh judgment I then passed upon her."* This sentiment has remained strong since then; in a later publication that came out in 1993 discussing Keats's *"Poetics, Letters, and Life"*, there is a chapter on Keats's love-letters to Fanny in which she is portrayed as a paragon among women, *"unsentimental, clear-sighted, frank, inquisitive, animated, kind, and invigorating. Her beauty resonated with the grace that comes of insight and deep abiding affection."*

John Evangelist Walsh presents a relatively more moderate assessment of Fanny. In his opinion, the letters, rather than completely doing away with what had been implied in Keats's letters to her, *"briefly illuminate another side of the girl's character, those quieter personal qualities which attracted Keats in the first place. Certainly the letters show her to have been, as Edgcumbe said, intelligent, observant, perceptive, though not unusually so, not to the "remarkable" extent perceived by their well-disposed editor."*

The changed perception of Fanny Brawne and her love for Keats had its reflection in the subsequent biographies of the poet as well as in other expressions of art depicting their love. Interestingly, therefore, Jane Campion's film "Bright Star" – about Keats's and Fanny's relationship – based on the 1997 Keats biography penned by Andrew Motion – portrays her as *"the steadfast Bright Star"* of Keats's sonnet; and it is Keats who is fickle, torn between his vocation, while she is witty, *"deeply kind and maternal"* --- an aspect of her character that became apparent from her letters to the poet's sister, Fanny Keats.

Did Fanny Brawne really care for the poetry of John Keats? She is dead, and cannot answer; but perhaps there is no doubt she loved John Keats the man. His poetry concerned her because it concerned him; she was born to love him.

As for Keats, with Fanny by his side he could put aside all his ambition and high ideals and philosophy for a little while. As he explained in a particularly eloquent letter written in March 1820 to Fanny:

> *"My Mind has been the most discontented and restless one that ever was put into a body too small for it. I never felt my Mind repose upon anything with complete and undistracted enjoyment – upon no person but you. When you are in the room my thoughts never fly out of window: you always concentrate my whole senses."*

Keats's love for Fanny was limitless. Love was his religion—he could die for it. His creed was love --- Fanny was its only tenet.

True to his words, John Keats died for love.

John Keats   Fanny Brawne

Fanny Brawne: A Tailpiece

After Keats's love letters to Fanny had been published in 1878, there was a general interest in Fanny Brawne. Subsequently, following publication of Fanny's letters to Keats's sister, Frances, in 1937, that brought out inner qualities of her mind and heart, a full biography of Fanny Brawne was much in demand. But when Herbert Lindon, the son of Fanny, was approached to sanction some publications concerning her, he refused; he gave his reasons. *"No doubt her life, in so far as it is connected with Keats, is more or less public property, but I think that this ceased to be the case when she married..."*

So the biography of Fanny Brawne had to wait. It was only later in 1952, her biography was written by the noted Keats scholar Joanna Richardson with unremitting enquiry, and imaginative sympathy.[211]

Whether through her thirty-two years of marriage Fanny was particularly happy or otherwise is an important question; but it is not decided even by Richardson's book, for much depended on the character of Louis Lindon, and not much is really known of him more than that in worldly affairs he was no great success.

---

[211] Richardson, Joanna: *"Fanny Brawne, a biography"*, Thames & Hudson, 1952.

Chapter 31
John Keats: Recognition after death

"There is a budding morrow in midnight."

-- John Keats

"To Autumn"

*"Season of mists and mellow fruitfulness,
Close bosom-friend of the maturing sun;
Conspiring with him how to load and bless
With fruit the vines that round the thatch-eves run;
To bend with apples the moss'd cottage-trees,
And fill all fruit with ripeness to the core;
To swell the gourd, and plump the hazel shells
With a sweet kernel; to set budding more,
And still more, later flowers for the bees,
Until they think warm days will never cease,
For summer has o'er-brimm'd their clammy cells."*

[John Keats, *"To Autumn"*]

In the years following his death, Keats's reputation grew steadily. "The Cambridge Apostles", a society of undergraduates that included Alfred Tennyson, a later Poet Laureate of England, was highly appreciative of his work. His influence is found everywhere in the decorative Romantic verse of the Victorian Age.

The first stanza of his poem *"To Autumn"* gave inspiration to the English author Neil Gaiman for his Sandman series, one of which is titled *"Season of the Mists"*.

"The Pre-Raphaelite Brotherhood of painters", an English group of well-known artists, was also inspired by the beauty and imagery of his poetry and illustrated it in their paintings. The first biography of Keats was published in 1848.

Today, Keats, who was once the victim of savage attack by a section of the contemporary critics, is considered one of the greatest English poets and is placed in the class of major English Romantic poets, like, Williams Wordsworth, Samuel Taylor Coleridge, William Blake, Lord Byron, and Percy Bysshe Shelley.

To mark the centenary anniversary of Keats's death, a *"John Keats Memorial Volume collection"* was brought out by the Keats House Committee, Hampstead on February 23, 1921. The collection comprises the original articles, essays, and poems written by prominent literary figures of the day as contributions to the "John Keats Memorial Volume", edited by G.C. Williamson. Included in the volume is a signed note by Thomas Hardy accompanying his poem *"At a House in Hampstead"*. Among the other literary persons who contributed are Henry van Dyke, General Sir Iain Hamilton, George Bernard Shaw, and Hugh Walpole. The collection also includes a publication illustrated with clippings, photographs, portraits, and signed autograph letters and notes by various literary persons regarding their willingness to contribute to the "John Keats Memorial Volume" – such as Arnold Bennett, John Galsworthy, H.G. Wells, A.E. Housman, Walter de la Mare, George Bernard Shaw, Osbert Sitwell, and John Drinkwater.

In 1973, "John Keats: His Life and Death", the first major motion picture about the life of Keats, directed by John Barnes, was produced by Encyclopaedia Britannica Inc. Later in 2009, the film "Bright Star", written and directed by Jan Campion, based on Keats's relationship with his love, Fanny Brawne was released.

"Keats-Shelley Memorial House", Rome

> *"An old-world house with rusted orange walls,*
> *Where, in the city's heart, you hear the drip*
> *Of Sabine waters plashing as it falls*
> *Into the marble semblance of a ship:*
> *Its windows open on a giant stair*
> *Crowded by an obelisk, and higher still*
> *Sun-traced in Rome's gold radiant air*

The Trinity that names the hill.
Enter the modest portal and ascend
Those narrow steps where once with labouring breath
He came at even and the journey's end
Who seeking life was greeted here by death
The marble stairs are steep, the shade strikes cold
In midmost summer. Fling the window open
And let the Roman Sun flood in. Behold
The place where Adonais died.
Little is changed. The lime-washed walls enclose
A narrow chamber, with a roof pale blue
Between the rafters, panelled for the rose
In mock relief that once his wide eyes knew,
Sleeplessly watching till the drooped lids tired:
A red-tiled floor, and windows whence at times
The lilt of the great city's life inspired
Suggestion of unwritten rhythms.
And this is all he knew of that great Rome,
The deathless mother of immortal men,
Dreamed of in visions in his Northern home,
And reached at last, and still beyond his ken:
A window world – blue noon and even's glow,
The passing pageant of the Spanish Square,
And blown from baskets on the steps below
The scent of violets in the air...."

["*The Keats-Shelly House in Rome, 1909*"]

On 23 February 1821, Keats died of tuberculosis in Rome. The walls of the house where he died were scraped and all things remaining in the room immediately burned (in accordance with the health laws of 19th century Rome) following the poet's death. There was a proposal for demolition of the house in the early 1900s.

An effort to purchase and restore the two-room apartment in which Keats spent his final days began in 1903 at the initiative of the American poet Robert Underwood Johnson. With the help and support of interested parties from America, England, and Italy, the house was purchased late in 1906 and dedicated in April 1909 for use by the *Keats–Shelley Memorial Association*; and since then it came to be known as the "*Keats–Shelley House*".

"Keats–Shelley House", Piazza di Spagna, Rome

Today at the foot of the steps of Piazza di Spagna in Rome, a door of an eighteenth-century building opens to introduce you to the most romantic of stories written by poets: their life! This is the "Keats–Shelley House" – a silent witness of the last hundred days of the mortal life of John Keats – now a writers' house museum, fascinating and evocative, that preserves the memory and the history of extraordinary and **vibrant** lives of the two poet friends John Keats and Percy Bysshe Shelley and several other renowned poets of the Romantic era.

"Keats–Shelley House", Piazza di Spagna, Rome

During World War II

During World War II, the Keats–Shelley House went "underground", especially after 1943, to secure its invaluable contents from falling into the hands of, and most likely being deliberately destroyed by, Nazi Germany. External markings relating to the museum were removed from the building. Although the library's 10,000 volumes were not removed, two boxes of artefacts were sent to the Abbey of Monte Cassino in December 1942 for safekeeping.

In October, 1943, the abbey's archivist placed the two unlabelled boxes of Keats–Shelley memorabilia with his personal possessions so that they could be removed during the abbey's evacuation and do not fall into the hands of the Germans. The items were later reclaimed by the museum's curator and returned to the Keats–Shelley House. The boxes were reopened in June 1944 upon the arrival of the Allied forces in Rome.

"Keats–Shelley House", Piazza di Spagna, Rome

The "Keats–Shelley House" has one of the world's most extensive collections of **paintings and portraits, busts and miniatures, relics and first editions,** memorabilia, **manuscripts and letters** relating to Keats and Shelley, as well as Lord Byron, Wordsworth, Robert Browning, Elizabeth Barett Browning, Oscar Wilde and others. It also houses an extensive library which has proved invaluable to many scholars and writers over the years.

"Keats–Shelley House", Piazza di Spagna, Rome

The rooms of the "Keats–Shelley House", fully furnished, preserve the atmosphere of a bygone era … time seems to have crystallized here! The collections include, inter alia, the immortal remains in Keats's verses as well as the first editions of his works. The letters Keats wrote to his *"shining star"* – Fanny Brawne – reflecting the nostalgia of distance until extreme separation, have all been carefully preserved. The piano melodies of his friend Severn resound here. The collections also include Severn's study of the dying Keats as well as his portrait of Shelley sitting among the ruins; and numerous other paintings, prints, furniture, sculptures, letters to friends and acquaintances. In addition, the museum houses **one of the finest libraries on Romantic literature in the world; there is also a small cinema hall where visitors can watch an exclusive introductory film about the Romantics.**

"Keats–Shelley House", Piazza di Spagna, Rome

"Keats-Shelly House is less of a museum than a house of contemplation" – Sedgewick of New York Times wrote way back in June, 1944. He was so right; for it is *"itself brooding inwardly upon its tenant the poet who died in one of its rooms about a century and a quarter before, and outwardly upon the very view which was before his eyes during the last days of his sad life"*.[212]

It is the place where ordained by destiny, Keats came, much against his wishes, leaving his near and dear ones – with hope to recover, return and reunite – but could not escape death. But till the end, he remained dedicated to pursuit of beauty and love – he died with love in his eyes.

---

[212] Sedgewick, A.C.: *"The Memorial Stands, Rome: June, 1944"*, published in "Keats, Shelley & Rome: An Illustrated Miscellany" edited by Neville Rogers (ed.,), Haskel House Publishers Ltd., Publishers of Scarce Scholarly Books, New York, N.Y., 1975.

Chapter 32
Epilogue

"Thou wast not born for death, immortal bird!
No hungry generations tread thee down;
The voice I hear this passing night was heard
In ancient days by emperor and clown."

-- John Keats, "Ode to a Nightingale"

In remembrance

In 1976, one hundred and fifty-five years after Keats's death, the International Astronomical Union (IAU), in a rare gesture of honour, has named one of Mercury's craters as "John Keats".

Mercury Crater -"John Keats"

The International Astronomical Union is responsible for naming celestial bodies, features, and other objects in space. Craters on planets and moons are commonly named after figures from various fields, including science, arts, and literature, as well as historical and cultural figures who have left a significant impact on humanity. The naming of Mercury's crater "John Keats" in 1976 signifies the recognition of Keats's contribution to literature and the arts. This gesture is particularly notable for it connects the realm of science with the realm of art, and acknowledges that the pursuit of knowledge through astronomy and space exploration is inherently linked to the exploration of human emotions, culture, and creativity.

In conclusion, the naming of a crater on Mercury after John Keats represents a unique and rare honour bestowed by the International Astronomical Union for it serves to immortalize his memory beyond Earth. Contrary to, therefore, what the poet thought of himself at the time of his death – that he was merely one whose name was writ in water, this rare distinction signifies the enduring impact of Keats's poetry and his contributions to human culture, bridging the gap between the arts and the sciences, and immortalizing his memory in the exploration of space.

References

1. "*Adonis*", Shelley's Poems, CliffsNotes
2. Bate, Walter Jackson: "*John Keats*", Cambridge, Mass.: Harvard University Press, 1964.
3. Bate, Walter Jackson. "*The Stylistic Development of Keats*", New York: Humanities Press, 1962.
4. Blackstone, Bernard. "*The Consecrated Urn*", Longmans Green: London (1959).
5. Bloom, Harold. "*The Visionary Company*", Ithaca: Cornell University Press, 1993, p.399.
6. Brock, R. C.: "*John Keats and Joseph Severn: The Tragedy of the Last Illness*", London: Keats-Shelley Memorial Association, 1973, p.18.
7. Brown, Charles Armitage: "*Letter of 7 August 1818*", in "The Life of John Keats", ed. London: Oxford University Press, 1937.
8. Brown, Charles Armitage (edited by Dorothy Hyde Bodurtha and W. B. Pope): "*The Life of John Keats*", Oxford University Press, London, 1937.
9. Brown, Sue: "*Joseph Severn, a Life: The Rewards of Friendship*", Oxford: Oxford University Press, 2009.
10. Bush, Douglas. "*John Keats: His Life and Writings*", London: Macmillan, 1966, p.148.
11. Campbell, Killis. "*The Origins of Poe*", The Mind of Poe and Other Studies. New York: Russell & Russell, Inc., 1962, pp. 154–155.
12. Castelow, Ellen: "*Eve of St. Agnes*", Historic UK.
13. Colvin, Sidney. "*John Keats: His Life and Poetry, His Friends, Critics and After-Fame*", London: Macmillan, 1917.
14. Colvin, Sydney: "*Keats*", Palala Press, 24 February 2018
15. Dawkins, Richard: "*Unweaving the Rainbow*", Boston, Mass.: Houghton Mifflin. Passim, 1998.

16. *"Don't give up the day job, Keats: how the poetic greats were snubbed"*, 23 August, 2021. https://shorturl.at/prMZ6
17. Edgcumbe, Fred (Ed): *"The Letters of Fanny Brawne to Fanny Keats, 1820-1824"*, Oxford University Press, H. Milford, 1936.
18. Edward MacDowell. *Lamia*, Op.29, score at IMSLP.
19. Encyclopedia Britannica.
20. Everest, Kelvin: "*Keats, John (1795–1821)*", Oxford Dictionary of National Biography, Oxford University Press, 2004 Online.
21. Evert, Walter: *"Aesthetics and Myth in the Poetry of Keats"*, Princeton: Princeton University Press, 1965, p.305.
22. Feynman, Richard: "*The Relation of Physics to Other Sciences*" Six Easy Pieces: Essentials of Physics Explained by Its Most Brilliant Teacher, 1995.
23. Fitzsimons, Eleanor: *"Wilde About Keats"*, Wordsworth Grasmere, 29 October, 2015. https://wordsworth.org.uk/blog/2015/10/29/wilde-about-keats/
24. Flood, Alison: *"Doctor's mistakes to blame for Keats's agonising end, says new biography"*, The Guardian, 26 Oct 2009.
25. Forman, H. Buxton (ed.), *"Poetical Works of John Keats"*, Crowell publ., 1895
26. Gittings, Robert: *"John Keats"*, London: Heinemann, 1968.
27. Gittings, Robert: *"Selected poems and letters of Keats"*, London: Heinemann, 1987, pp. 1-3.
28. Gittings, Robert: "The odes of Keats and their earliest known manuscripts in Facsimile", Kent State University Press, 1970.
29. Hanson, Marilee. "*John Keats Letter To Benjamin Bailey, 10 June 1818*", English History, March 17, 2015
30. *"How close were Shelley and Keats?"*, The Irish Times, November 20, 2009.
31. Hughes, Sean P. & Snell, Noel: ""*Is the Criticism of John Keats's Doctors Justified? A Bicentenary Re-Appraisa*l", Taylor & Francis Online, Published online: 23 Jun 2021, pp. 41-55.
32. *"Hyperion: work by Keats"*, Encyclopedia Britannica.

33. Internet Archive. https://archive.org/details/aclassicaldicti00lempgoog
34. Jarcho, Saul: "Amy Lowell and the Death of John Keats", Clio Medica, Vol. 12, No.1, pp. 91-95, 1977.
35. "*John Keats*": The Oxford Companion to English Literature. Edited by Dinah Birch.
36. "*John Keats*", Poemhunters.com
37. "*John Keats and His Ten Day Quarantine*", Cove. https://shorturl.at/gmxBI
38. "*John Keats and Keats's Odes Background*", in 'Keats's Odes', Sparknotes.
39. "*John Keats (1795-1821), Life Mask by Benjamin Robert Haydon (1786-1846)*", TREGEAGLE. https://shorturl.at/acAJW
40. Keats, John: "*The complete poetical works and letters of John Keats*", Cambridge Edition, Boston and New York, Houghton, Mifflin and Company, The University Press, Cambridge, 1899.
41. Keats, John: "*Bright Star: Love Letters and Poems of John Keats to Fanny Brawne*", Penguin Books; Media Tie In edition, 16 September 2009.
42. Keats, John, "*The Life and Letters of John Keats*", ed. Richard Houghton (reprint). Read Books, 2008. p.162.
43. "*Keats's Odes*", British Literature Wiki.
44. Kirk, Naomi J.: "*The Girl who shared Keats's Fate: "In Praise of Lady Dead and—"*", American Scholar, 6 (1937), p. 49.
45. "*Letter from Lord Byron to John Murray about the death of Keats, 26 April 1821*", Collection items, British Library. https://shorturl.at/lFWX9.
46. "*Letter #183: To Fanny Brawne, 4 (?) Feb 1820*", The Keats Letters Project, February 4, 2020. https://shorturl.at/fiJZ5
47. "*11 December 1816: Meeting Percy Shelley: Joined but not Close*", Mapping Keats's Progress: A Critical Chronology. https://shorturl.at/ptSZ7

48. *"12 August, 1820: Keats: "Excessively Nervous" & "Cheating the Consumption"*, Mapping Keats's Progress: A Critical Chronology. https://shorturl.at/jmnvN

49. Laennec, R.: *"A Treatise on the Diseases of the Chest and on Mediate Auscultation"*, 4th edition, London: Longman, 1834, p.331.

50. Letter to Sarah Jeffrey'. 9 June 1819. Colvin 1970 qtd. p. 356.

51. Lloyd, Andrew: *"Writ in water, preserved in plaster: how Keats' death mask became a collector's item"*, The Guardian, 26 Feb 2021.

52. Lounis Nacer, Caroline Maslo, Johan R. Boelaert, Chantal Truffot-Pernot, Ji Baohong, Jacques Grosset, *"Impact of iron loading and iron chelation on murine tuberculosis,"* Clinical Microbiology and Infection, Vol. 5, No. 11 (1999): pp. 687–92;

53. Lounis Nacer, Chantal Truffot-Pernot, Jacques Grosset, Victor R. Gordeuk, Johan R. Boelaert, *"Iron and Mycobacterium tuberculosis infection,"* Journal of Clinical Virology, Vol. 20 No. 3 (2001): pp. 123–6.

54. Lovell Jr., Ernest J: *"Captain Medwin: Friend of Byron and Shelley"*, University of Texas, 1962.

55. Lowell, Amy: *"John Keats"*, Boston, Houghton Mifflin Company, 1925.

56. Malone, Peter: '*Keats's "Posthumous Existence" in Plaster*', The Keats-Shelley Review, vol. 26, 2012, pp.125-35.

57. Marchand, Leslie A.(ed.): "*Born for Opposition*": Byron's Letters and Journals, Vol. 8: 1821, London: John Murray, 1978.

58. McGann, Jerome: "*Keats and the Historical Method in Literary Criticism*", MLN 94 (1979), pp. 988–989.

59. Mercer Anna: *"On This Day: 9 October 1816, John Keats and Leigh Hunt"*, Bar's Blog, October 9, 2016.

60. Miller, Lucasta: "Keats: A Brief Life in Nine Poems and One Epitaph", Vintage Digital, 4 February 2021.

61. Milnes, Richard Monckton (ed.): *"The Life, Letters, and Literary Remains of John Keats"*, London, Edward Moxon, Dover Street, 1848.

62. Mirza, Shikoh Mohsin: "*Poetry of the Soul: The Sublime and Wondrous Odes of John Keats*", Wire, July 17, 2021. https://shorturl.at/lwBE6
63. Mondlin, Marvin & Meador, Roy: "*Book Row: An Anecdotal & Pictorial History*", Carroll & Graf Publishers, 2004.
64. Montague, John: "*A poet pursued by death*", Irish Times, October 20, 2012
65. Moses, Henry: "*A Collection of Antique Vases, Altars, Paterae, Tripods, Candelabra Sarcophagi, etc.*", J. Taylor London, c.1823.
66. Motion, Andrew: "*Keats*", London: Faber, 1997.
67. Mythili S & Suganya, John M.: "*The Real and Ideal World in The Odes of John Keats*", Journal of Emerging Technologies and Innovative Research (JETIR), Volume 8, Issue 12, December 2021
68. Pinsky, Robert: "*A Poet's Poet: The Astonishing Career of John Keats*", The New York Times, April 15, 2022.
69. Popova, Maria: "*Ode to a Flower: Richard Feynman's Famous Monologue on Knowledge and Mystery, Animated*", The Marginalian.
70. Popova, Maria: "*The World's Most Lyrical Footnote: Physicist Richard Feynman on the Life-Expanding Common Ground Between the Scientific and the Poetic Worldviews*", Marginalian.
71. Reynolds, Ian: "*The Gravestone of John Keats: Romancing the Stone*", Wordsworth Grasmere, 16 April, 2018. https://shorturl.at/fyCTU
72. "*Richard Feynman's 'Ode To A Flower' quote, animated*", TKSST (The Kid Should See This), https://shorturl.at/iTV28
73. Richardson, Joanna. "*Fanny Brawne: A Biography*", Norwich: Jarrold and Sons, 1952.
74. Ricks, Christopher: "Keats, Byron, and 'Slippery Blisses", Chapter IV in "*Keats and Embarrassment*", published by Oxford University Press. 1 March, 1984.
75. Roe, Nicholas: "*John Keats- A New Life*", Yale University Press, 2013.
76. Rollins, Hyder E.: "*The Keats Circle: Letters and Papers 1816-78*", ed. Hyder E. Rollins Harvard, 2nd edition, 1965.

77. Rollins, Hyder E.: *"The Keats Circle, Letters and Papers 1816–1878, and More Letters and Poems, 1814–1879"*, ed. Hyder Edward Rollins, 2 vols., Cambridge, MA: Harvard University Press, 1969, I, p. 163.
78. Schuster, M. Lincoln: *"The World's Great Letters"*, Simon & Schuster, New York, 1940.
79. Sedgewick, A.C.: *"The Memorial Stands, Rome: June, 1944"*, published in "Keats, Shelley & Rome: An Illustrated Miscellany" edited by Neville Rogers (ed.,), Haskel House Publishers Ltd., Publishers of Scarce Scholarly Books, New York, N.Y., 1975.
80. *"Selections from Keats's Letters"*, Poetry Foundation.
81. Selincourt, Ernest de: *"The Poems of John Keats"*, London, 1951, p. 576.
82. Smith, Hillas: *"Keats and Medicine"*, Newport, Isle of Wight: Cross Publishing, 1995), pp. 110–11.
83. Sperry, Stuart: *"Keats the Poet"*, Princeton: Princeton University Press, 1973, p.288.
84. Spivey Nicole, Uffelman Lindsay, Keeports Katie, Grewal Ann: *"Keats's Letters"*, British Literature Wiki.
85. *"Study Guide: John Keats Childhood"* https://shorturl.at/stwLP
86. Tearle, Oliver: *"The True Meaning of Keats's 'Beauty is Truth, Truth Beauty'"*, Interesting Literature.
87. *"The Eve of St. Agnes: Poem by John Keats – Analysis"*, Literature Analysis. https://t.ly/u2PYM
88. The Oxford Companion to English Literature: "*John Keats*", edited by Dinah Birch.
89. Vendler, Helen. *"The Odes of John Keats"*. Cambridge, Massachusetts: Harvard University Press, 1983, p. 20.
90. Walsh, John Evangelist. *"Darkling, I Listen: The Last Days and Death of John Keats"*, New York: St. Martin's Press, 1999.
91. Ward, Aileen: *"The Date of Keats's "Bright Star" Sonnet"*, Studies in Philology, Vol. 52, No. 1 (Jan., 1955), University of North Carolina Press, p. 75-85.

92. Watts, Cedric Thomas: *"A preface to Keats"*, Longman, University of Michigan, 1985, p. 90.
93. Wells, Walter: *"A Doctor's Life of John Keats"*, New York: Vantage, 1959, p. 209.
94. *"What is flunkeyism in W. M. Thackeray's works and Miltonic inversion in Paradise Lost?"*, e-notes.
95. White, R.S. *"John Keats: A Literary Life"*. Palgrave Macmillan, 2010, p.146.
96. *"Why John Keats's Hyperion is Called a Fragment?"*, published in 'Ask literature', November 9, 2018.
97. Wikipedia
98. Wright, Brooks: "*On the Sale by Auction of Keats's Love Letters*": *A Footnote to Wilde's Sonnet,* Keats-Shelley Journal, Vol. 7 (Winter, 1958), p. 9-11.

----

www.ingramcontent.com/pod-product-compliance
Lightning Source LLC
LaVergne TN
LVHW061542070526
838199LV00077B/6873